Why Me, Lord?

To James
from
Aunt Anna - '86

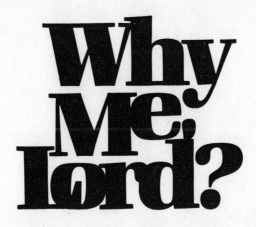

Why Me, Lord?

Paul W. Powell

This book is designed for your personal reading pleasure and profit. It is also designed for group study. A leader's guide with helps and hints for teachers and visual aids (Victor Multiuse Transparency Masters) is available from your local bookstore or from the publisher.

VICTOR
V.®
BOOKS a division of SP Publications, Inc.
WHEATON, ILLINOIS 60187

Offices also in
Whitby, Ontario, Canada
Amersham-on-the-Hill, Bucks, England

Fourth printing, 1985

Recommended Dewey Decimal Classification: 241.1
Suggested subject heading: THE WILL OF GOD IN CRISES

Library of Congress Catalog Card Number 80-52947
ISBN: 0-89693-007-6

VICTOR BOOKS
A division of SP Publications, Inc.
Wheaton, Illinois 60187

Dedication

To the women in my life:
Mary, my mother
Emma, Pat, and Lillian, my sisters
Cathy, my wife
Lori, my daughter
Gerrie, my editor
Gloria, my secretary
Anita, my typist

Contents

Preface

How to live! How to die! We all need to know how to do that. Death is the common enemy of us all. It entered the world as a result of Adam's sin and has since passed on to all men. Death is a part of life. Sooner or later it comes to all of us. Not even the only begotten Son of God escaped it. The Prophet Isaiah tells us even Jesus was "a Man of sorrows, and acquainted with grief" (Isa. 53:3). We do not live long before we become "acquainted with grief" also.

Sickness and suffering are even more common than death. Their presence and prevalence are found throughout the pages of Scripture, the pages of history, and the pages of today's newspaper. Job was right: "Man that is born of a woman is of few days and full of trouble" (Job 14:1).

To live victoriously then, we must have a faith to live by and a faith to die by. We must learn how to deal constructively with both the sufferings of life and the sorrows of death. We must learn how to live and how to die.

That's the purpose of this book. These pages contain answers, attitudes, and actions that I have found to be helpful in handling both life and death. They are presented here with the hope that they will help you also.

Naturally, I owe a debt of gratitude to scores of teachers, authors, preachers, and friends who have touched my life through the years. Particular appreciation is due Gerrie Milburn for editing the manuscript, and to my secretary Gloria Ortega and my friend Anita Anderson for typing it.

Part I
How to Live

ONE

Why?
Why?
Why?

Don Anthony was a great Christian who died triumphantly. But before his final victory, he had to grapple with the mystery of suffering. His struggle started one summer when he began having digestive problems. When the difficulties persisted, he sought medical help. His physician referred him to Scott and White Hospital in Temple, Texas for more extensive examination. Doctors there recommended exploratory surgery and warned him to expect the worst.

The surgery revealed an inoperable and incurable malignancy. Apart from a miracle, he was told, he had only about a year to live.

A few days later I visited with him, and he shared with me the struggle he was going through. Like most of us he had always assumed that he would live to a ripe old age and then die peacefully in his sleep. He could not understand why he should suddenly be afflicted with a deadly disease while still in his 40s.

He was the father of two teenaged children. The thought of not seeing them grow up distressed him. He did not know how he could cope with leaving them at such a critical time in their lives.

Don believed that God had led him to his new position as director of Christian education for Texas Baptists. He had just

13

recently completed long-range plans that would require his careful coordination in order to make them successful. He did not understand why God would lead him to this position and then allow such an illness to befall him, just when his work was beginning to bear fruit. And most of all he wondered, if he were to suffer a prolonged illness, how he could learn to cope on a day-to-day basis with the pain, weakness, and discouragement he would surely experience. Don was struggling with the basic question of all sufferers: Why?

This question has baffled the minds of wise men, philosophers, and saints throughout the ages. The continuation of diseases, wars, accidents, famine, and pestilence perplexes us. We wonder why God doesn't step in and put an end to such things.

There is no easy answer. The late Senator Thomas Hart Benton of Missouri used to talk about a disease called "the simples." He was referring to the process of giving simple answers to the hard problems of life.

Experience and study of the Scriptures have taught me to avoid "the simples" when trying to explain suffering. To blame everything on God is too easy. To label every experience as "the will of God" or the work of the devil is too simple. The problem is far more complex than that.

While the answer as to why people suffer is not easy to come by, inquiring minds and aching hearts demand some explanation for it. So I shared with Don the following reasons why I believe people suffer.

Judgment on Sin

The oldest and most common explanation for suffering is that it comes from God as punishment for sin. This idea is more deeply imbedded in most of us than we realize. A lawyer friend of mine began having severe headaches. When the usual medications didn't help, he went to his physician. The doctor's initial diagnosis was a tumor in the brain, but he wanted a further examination at John Sealy Hospital in Galveston. The tests there confirmed the doctor's worst fears. It was a tumor that required immediate surgery. The doctors told him that he might not come out of surgery alive.

Charles asked me to visit him before surgery, so I flew down to be with him and his family. When we were alone, he said, "I wonder what I've done to deserve this? I didn't think I had been that bad." Unconsciously, he was expressing the belief that all suffering comes from God as punishment for sin. He believed that since he had cancer he must have committed some great sin, and he just didn't know what it was.

This idea was the most common explanation for suffering in the Old Testament days. The Book of Job is probably the oldest book in the Bible. It is the story of a righteous man who lost his family, his wealth, and his health. Three of his friends came to be with him and comfort him in his misery. They expressed the common belief of their day when one of them asked Job, "Whoever perished being innocent? Or where were the righteous cut off?" (Job 4:7) If Job was having a bad time, they felt it was because he had been bad. They believed all suffering was due to sin.

This prevalent belief about suffering persisted in Jesus' day. The disciples once talked with Jesus about a man born blind. They asked, "Who did sin, this man, or his parents, that he was born blind?" (John 9:2) They were sure his blindness was due to sin. Their only question was, "*Whose* sin?" This explanation for suffering still prevails today.

True, some suffering is due to God's judgment on sin. The Flood came in Noah's day because of people's wickedness. Amos said that famine, pestilence, earthquakes, and even defeat in battle were due to Israel's sin. And the Apostle Paul teaches that we reap what we sow (Gal. 6:7). We live in a moral universe and we can't go against the grain without getting splinters.

However, Jesus categorically rejected this as the only explanation for suffering. In response to the question of His disciples about whose sin had caused the man's blindness, Jesus answered in effect, "Nobody's" (John 9:1-3). Jesus clearly affirmed that some suffering has absolutely no relationship to sin or character.

So *some* judgment comes on sin here and now, and with it comes suffering of all kinds. But primarily the judgment of God is reserved until the end of time (Matt. 13:18-43).

Chastisement of God

Another explanation for suffering is that it comes as a chastisement from God. This is closely related to the idea of judgment, but it's not the same. Suffering and affliction that comes from God is not to punish us, but to discipline us so we'll get closer to Him.

This too is a basic teaching of Scripture (Heb. 12:5-15). Chastisement is pictured as a sign of God's love and of our genuine sonship. If God loves us as His children, He must, like a father, discipline us to bring us to maturity. If there is no discipline, it is because we are not His children.

As a parent I have found it necessary to discipline my children often. I've refused them, grounded them, fussed at them, and even spanked them. This is never easy for me. In fact it often hurts me more than it hurts them. But it is necessary. They seemingly will not learn any other way, and I love them too much to let them go uncorrected. I want them to develop into mature, whole, happy people. And love requires that I chasten them.

God is the same way. If we are His children, we can expect to be corrected and even punished. He loves us too much to let us do wrong without correcting us.

God uses all kinds of experiences to chasten His children. He uses weakness, sickness, and even death (1 Cor. 11:30-32). The Christians in Corinth were guilty of not showing proper respect in remembering the Lord's body and blood. They were turning the Lord's Supper into a drunken brawl. God sent weakness, sickness, and death to correct them. That's right—even death! Apparently at times God will even take His children out of the world immediately, rather than allow them to go on in their sin (1 John 5:16).

Attacks from Satan

The most logical explanation for suffering is often overlooked. It is that suffering comes from Satan in an effort to destroy our faith. Satan is alive and active on Planet Earth, and he has tremendous power. It is ultimately limited by God, but it is still great. One who blames all suffering on God completely ignores Satan's existence and work.

Biblical writers often blame suffering and sickness on the devil. Jesus referred to a lady who had been crippled 18 years as one "whom Satan hath bound" (Luke 13:16).

Paul spoke of having a thorn in the flesh. He described it as "the messenger of Satan" to torment him (2 Cor. 12:7-10). He believed that Satan, not God, was the author of this infirmity that kept plaguing him.

Job also experienced suffering that came from Satan. The writer of the Book of Job tells how Satan appeared before God to accuse Job of serving God only for what he could get out of Him. When Satan persisted in his argument, God allowed him to test Job's faith.

So Satan sent a tornado that killed all of Job's children. He sent robbers who stole all of Job's wealth. Finally, he sent boils to afflict Job's body.

None of this suffering came from God. It all came from Satan. And it didn't come because Job was bad. It came because he was good. It was an effort on Satan's part to drive Job to despair. It was designed to get him to curse God and die. This is also true of much of our suffering.

God is not the author of suffering and evil. Calamity is not His handiwork. Disease is not His making. These evils are not His will or design. Do you doubt this? Look at the story of Creation. Originally there was no disease, disaster, deformity, or death in the world. These came only after Adam and Eve sinned (Gen. 3:17-19) and tells us something about God's ideal world before the Fall.

Look at the end of time. In heaven there will be no tears, no sorrow, no pain, and no death (Rev. 21:4); this shows that evil and suffering are not God's perfect will for us.

If this is not enough evidence, look at the life and ministry of Jesus. A great part of Christ's time on earth was spent in healing the sick and diseased. Never once did He turn someone away, saying, "I'm sorry, friend. I cannot heal you because God wants you to suffer."

Jesus looked on disease and death as intruders and aliens in

God's kingdom. He did not regard God as their author. Neither should we.

So the next time sickness, suffering, or tragedy hits you or someone you love, don't be sure that God sent it. Instead of asking, "Why has God done this?" you might ask, "Did Satan do this?" And if you wonder, "What have I done to deserve this?" the answer might well be, "Nothing. Nothing at all."

Much suffering is the work of Satan, to drive God's people to despair and rejection. When God chastens His children, He does so to make them better, but Satan attacks them to make them bitter.

Freedom of Choice

Another cause of suffering is our free will. Basic to the question of evil and suffering is the question, "Why did God create us in the first place?" He created us to share His joy. He wants us to enjoy life as He enjoys it. But this calls for our being free to make choices. If God had not given us His kind of freedom, we could not experience His kind of joy. So God created us with the ability to make our own choices. With this gift comes both a risk and a responsibility.

We all have the privilege and power of choice. As the Prophet Isaiah says, "Man chooses his own ways" (Isa. 66:3, author's paraphrase). This means we can choose to walk with God or walk away from Him. We may obey his Word or violate it. We are free to make mistakes and to do foolish and careless things. We are free to sin. Much suffering results from our abusing God's gift of freedom.

Let me illustrate. God created a universe governed by laws, such as the law of gravity. If we live in harmony with these laws, we prosper. If we conflict with them, we suffer. The choice is ours. Gravity holds our world together. Without it things would fly apart. So gravity is good. But if we ignore it and step off a high cliff, it may pull us to our death.

We are also free to sin. We car get drunk, drive a car, and kill an innocent child. When this happens, we shouldn't say it's "the will of God." The statute books call it a crime. If we call it otherwise, we are blaming God for things we condemn people for. Such an act is not the will of God. It results from the sinful will of man. We shouldn't ask *God*, "Why?" Instead, we should ask the *drunk*, "Why?" He made the choice. God is to blame only in that He allows us to make our own choices.

We live in a world where nobody lives to himself and nobody dies to himself. The good others do splashes on us. Aren't we glad of that?

But the opposite is also true. The evil people do splashes on us too. Much suffering is due to our own mistakes and carelessness and the sins of others. Suffering may not be related to our character at all.

Only indirectly then is God responsible for such suffering. If we are going to blame God for anything, we ought to blame Him for loving us and trusting us too much, not too little. He wanted us to taste His joy of life and obviously felt it was worth the risk. In a sense we can blame Him for starting the whole process, but it is not His fault that we have done what we have done. The fault is not the Creator's. It is the creature's. The flaws are ours, not His.

World in Travail

Finally, there is much suffering that cannot be blamed on the judgment of God, Satan, or the freedom of man. Such things as floods, storms, earthquakes, cancer, and deformities are often beyond our control. They happen to both the guilty and the innocent. They don't appear to be acts of judgment, chastisement, or the results of our choices. Then why do they come? They come as a result of a world under the curse of sin—a world in travail.

Tragedy, suffering, and death were not a part of God's original creation. These entered as a result of sin, and when human nature fell, the physical nature fell also (Gen. 3:17-19). Few of us realize the far-reaching effects of sin on the natural order. When Adam and Eve sinned, all kinds of evil forces were unloosed on the earth. All creation was infected by the sins of people. This probably accounts for most natural calamities that are labeled "acts of God."

The Apostle Paul tells us that the state of the earth is as bad as the state of man. God says that all creation groans for redemption (Romans 8:22). This means that the physical order is under the curse of sin, as humans are. And God's final redemption will not only include man, but also heaven and earth (2 Peter 3:13).

Storms, famine, pestilence, and volcanoes are just the groans and sighs of nature. Man's sin put thorns on roses, fierceness in beasts, and storms in the wind. Much suffering then is simply the price we pay for living in this world, which is under the curse of sin.

It is like walking into the isolation ward of a hospital. No matter how healthy you are, there is a risk involved. The problem is not your health, but the germ-infested environment. To enter is to expose yourself to danger.

There is a risk involved in living in this sin-infested world. If you are in the wrong place at the wrong time, you may suffer from sin's effects. Such suffering may have nothing whatever to do with the kind of life you have lived. It is just a part of the risk of being alive on Planet Earth after sin cursed it.

So suffering comes for many reasons. Some comes from God's judgment of sin; some comes as chastisement to correct and develop us; some comes from Satan to destroy our faith; some comes because of our own carelessness or foolishness; some comes because of the sins of others; and some comes just because we live in a sin-infested world.

As you can see, there is no simple answer as to why we suffer. And when we have learned all we can about suffering, we still may not know why it comes in any one particular instance. This may remain a mystery as long as we live.

Since we do not know all the whys of suffering, we should take the stance of faith and humility before it. Like Job, who did not understand at first why all those things were happening to him, we should say, "Though He slay me, yet will I trust in Him" (Job 13:15). Like Jesus, who did not understand why He was being forsaken on the cross (Matt. 27:46), we should still say, "Father, into Thy hands I commend My spirit" (Luke 23:46).

This is not blind fatalism. This is Christian optimism. Paul learned through his suffering that God's grace is sufficient (2 Cor. 12:9). God's grace is enough for you too. If you keep trusting the Lord, even though you can't understand all the whys of life, you will find this to be true. Then no matter why suffering comes, you will live and die as a better person.

TWO

The Choice Is Yours

The most important thing about suffering is not why it happens, but how we respond to it. Attitudes, not answers, are the key to triumphant living.

To know why suffering comes does not ease its pain or heal its hurt. But if we respond to it correctly, we can be made better by it, regardless of its cause.

How we respond to suffering is entirely up to us. We do not get to choose many experiences in life. Though we may never understand why some things happen, we can choose our responses to them. We can determine how experiences affect our lives by our attitudes.

We are like the young man who sold books from house to house. He was lame and walked with great difficulty. At one house where he stopped, the lady rudely turned him down. When he started away, she saw his condition and called him back. "I didn't know you were lame," she said. "I will buy a book."

But he wasn't selling sympathy. He was selling books, and he let her know it.

She said, "Doesn't being lame color your life?"

He replied, "Yes, but thank God I can choose the color." So

can we. Troubles do color our lives, but we get to choose their color.

There are at least five responses we can make to suffering.

Bitterness

The first is bitterness. We can follow the advice that Job's wife gave him in his suffering. We can "curse God, and die" (Job. 2:9).

Sometimes even people who claim they don't believe in God do this. As actor Dean Jones told about his conversion, he explained his attitude toward all the earlier troubles he had gone through in his life. He said, "I had quit believing in God, but I had not quit blaming God."

This is how even some Christians respond to suffering. They blame God for everything that happens to them and become resentful, skeptical, and unbelieving.

What a tragedy! What good does bitterness do? It doesn't change the situation. It doesn't take away the hurt. It doesn't give life more meaning. All that bitterness changes is the people it engulfs. It makes them sullen, sour, and unpleasant.

If we become bitter, we are looking at only one side of life. If evil and suffering cause us to question God, then goodness should cause us to affirm God. We should not question the existence of evil and suffering and take for granted the presence of good. We should be consistent. If one demands an explanation, so does the other. If evil and suffering make it hard to believe in God, then good should make it hard not to believe in Him.

Arthur John Gossip once said, "Some people, when belief comes hard, fling away from the Christian faith altogether. But in heaven's name," he asked, speaking from the depths of personal disaster, "fling away for what?"

In the face of suffering, we are like the disciples who were asked by Jesus, "Will you also go away?"

They replied, "Lord, to whom shall we go? Thou hast the words of eternal life" (John 6:68).

In this life you either swim with Jesus or sink—in despair. Don't waste your time in bitterness. It takes too much energy and it accomplishes nothing.

Self-Pity

A second response we can make to our problems is self-pity. We can feel sorry for ourselves and cry, "Why me?"

Don't surrender to this negative attitude. Others have faced troubles and have overcome them to do marvelous things in life. You can do the same. Beethoven wrote some of his most beautiful music after he was completely deaf. John Milton wrote *Paradise Lost* after he became blind. Robert Louis Stevenson had tuberculosis. Franklin D. Roosevelt was crippled by polio and needed steel braces in order to stand, but this did not deter him from becoming president of the United States. Thomas Edison was almost deaf, but his genius as an inventor changed the course of history.

When Louis Braille was three years old, an accident in his father's workshop blinded him for life. He could have given up and quit struggling to live a productive life. However, by the age of 18 he had developed a system of reading for blind people which has helped millions who cannot see.

The Apostle Paul had a thorn in the flesh. What was it? We don't know. We have 13 letters written by him but the Spirit never led him to explain what his thorn was.

He did not want that thorn and he asked repeatedly that it be removed. But it wasn't and he had to live with it. So he got on with the main business of life. He had no time for self-pity.

The late Hubert H. Humphrey, senator from Minnesota and former Vice-President of the United States, was a man of boundless optimism and enthusiasm. Following cancer surgery he was given a slim chance to live more than five years. When someone expressed sympathy to him, he replied, "Oh, my friend, it isn't what they take from you that counts—it's what you do with what you have left."

Adversity is an experience, not a final act. Don't let it drive you either to despair or to self-pity. If these people under such mighty hardships could and did dare to do so much, why shouldn't you?

Unquestioned Resignation

A third response we can make to suffering is unquestioning res-
ignation. We can take the attitude that whatever will be will be.
Some people believe that we are to accept life without question.
They don't think we have a right to question God about anything.

I once preached a sermon on suffering in which I suggested that
we do have a right to question God. The next week a lady told me
she was shocked to hear me make such a statement. She thought no
one ever had a right to question God.

I reminded her that Habakkuk questioned God. He was the first
of Israel's religious skeptics. He saw the wicked prospering and
the righteous being trampled down in his day and he cried out to
God for an explanation. He wanted to know why this was happening (Hab. 1:3). And I added that even Jesus questioned God. On
the cross He cried, "My God, My God, why hast Thou forsaken
Me?" (Matt. 27:46)

The Bible teaches that God holds us responsible for our actions,
and I believe He expects us to hold Him responsible for His.
There's a lot that God can explain. Many graves in the cemetery
need to be explained. There is a lot of suffering and illness that
goes unexplained if we choose to bury our feelings and refuse to
learn from the sorrows of life.

While no answer may come immediately, it is not wrong for us
to ask God why things happen. He gave us minds. He expects us to
inquire into the meaning of life and suffering. Accepting life
without questions is failing to use the intelligence that God gave
us.

Total Intellectual Understanding

A fourth response we can make to suffering is to demand a total
intellectual understanding of all that happens. This is as unreason-
able as blind resignation. It is asking for more than God will
reveal. We can never understand the ways and thoughts of God
(Isa. 55:8-9). They are beyond our comprehension (Rom. 11:33).

Though there is an explanation of all suffering, our finite minds
cannot always comprehend it. In this life we must be content with a

limited understanding. We will not understand all things until we get to heaven (1 Cor. 13:12). To expect a total intellectual understanding of all of life now is to expect too much.

Faith

The best response we can make to suffering is to let it turn us to God in faith. Faith is looking to God for help and for hope. Faith is believing in His love and power enough to ask Him to help us. It is trusting in Him even when we do not understand why things have happened to us

Eloise Hammack had the kind of faith I'm talking about. She was a member of a church I once pastored. Several years ago I returned there to conduct a funeral. At the graveside Eloise told me she had just learned that she had cancer. Several years earlier she had gone through a cancer operation and a series of treatments and since then she had had no problems. She presumed she was cured. Then her problems recurred. The doctors advised her to enter the hospital for a complete examination. Naturally this distressed her. She said, "I was so worried and afraid that I could not sleep. I prayed and prayed and prayed until I came to the place where I could pray no more. Finally I said, 'Oh, God, whatever Your will is, I accept it.' And when I said that, there came to me a peace that I had never experienced before in my life."

When the final tests were in, her worst fear was confirmed. It was cancer in an advanced stage. She said, "But the peace was still there. I wasn't troubled. I wasn't upset. I wasn't worried. And when my friends came to visit me and saw how I was responding to this emotionally, they said, 'Eloise, we don't understand.' " Then she said, "You know, Paul, I don't understand it either. I think this must be the 'peace that passeth all understanding.' "

Eloise let her trouble turn her to God, and He gave her the strength and grace to live victoriously in spite of her illness.

He can do the same for us if we turn to Him.

Bitterness and self-pity can destroy us. Believing in blind fate or demanding total understanding can never satisfy us. But faith in the Lord can strengthen and sustain us.

Let your suffering turn you to God. Seek His face through prayer and Bible study. Ask Him to give you courage, strength, and peace. If you do, you will emerge from your suffering a wiser, braver, and better person.

THREE

Triumph Out of Tragedy

Faith is believing not only that God will help us in our suffering here and now, but also that He will bring something worthwhile out of it in the future.

That's the promise of Scripture. Paul declares, "We know that all things work together for good to them that love God, to them who are the called according to His purpose" (Rom. 8:28).

It is not God's purpose that we always enjoy lives of physical ease. He is more concerned about our spiritual development. His aim is not primarily that we be comfortable on earth but that we be "conformed to the image of His Son" (Rom. 8:29). His ultimate goal is to make us like Jesus Christ.

To this end, Paul says, God can and does use "all things" that happen to us. This does not mean God *causes* all things. He doesn't. And it doesn't mean that all things are good. They aren't. But it does mean that God can use all things—even those things that He doesn't cause and even bad things—to make us better people.

Rightly understood, this is the basis for profound optimism. It means that in spite of suffering and tragedy, God is never defeated or frustrated. He can bring victory out of defeat and triumph out of tragedy today, just as He did at Calvary. It means that no experience has to be a total waste for one of God's children. Regardless of what happens to us or why it happens, God can still use it to shape our character. It means that God can take the most severe suffering and use that to develop us into more mature, Christlike people.

Just as our Lord Jesus was made perfect (mature) through the things that He suffered, so we can be shaped, molded, and polished by sufferings (Heb. 2:10).

Look at some worthwhile things that can come from sorrow and suffering.

Patience

First, suffering can develop patience in us. Patience is the ability to stand up to the pressures of life without going to pieces or to tranquilizers. Patience helps develop the strength of character needed to live life victoriously.

Some of us feel that Christianity is a miracle drug that should make our lives easy, but it isn't. The purpose of Christianity is not to exempt us from difficulty, but to produce in us a character adequate to meet life as it comes. Being Christians makes us strong—not soft. It does not give us escape from life's burdens, but strengthens us for meeting them bravely.

Dr. Dan Poling, in his book *Faith Is Power* (Greenberg Publishers, pp. 29-30), tells of his son's departure for overseas duty as a chaplain during World War II. He said to his father, "Dad, I don't want you to pray for my return. Just pray that I shall never be a coward. Dad, pray that I shall be adequate." That's what God wants to do in our lives. He wants to make us adequate for whatever comes.

But how can God develop this adequacy in us? One way is through trials and difficulties. James wrote, "The trying of your faith worketh patience" (James 1:3). And Paul wrote, "Tribulation worketh patience" (Rom. 5:3). The only way God develops strength of character in us is to allow us to experience trials and difficulties.

There is an old adage in nautical circles to the effect that "No sailor ever distinguished himself on a smooth sea." This means that it takes difficulty and hardship to bring out human development and greatness. For some reason the full potential of a person never comes to the surface amid ease and comfort.

If a football coach wants to strengthen his players, he doesn't send them out to play with feather pillows. He sends them out against rough opponents and hard tackling dummies. Through struggle and strain they develop physical muscle. We develop strength of character, spiritual muscles, in a similar way.

So one worthwhile thing that can come from trouble is that it can develop patience in us. It can make us adequate to face life.

True Values

Second, suffering can teach us true values. The lawyer friend I mentioned in chapter 1 survived his operation for a brain tumor and lived for another year-and-a-half. He was even able to go back to his law practice for a few months. The last Sunday he was able to attend church, I asked him to share his testimony with our congregation. He told how going through this illness had changed his life. He said he had been only a nominal Christian and church member until the malignancy had appeared. Then everything changed. He said that he now looked at life, God, and his family in an entirely different light. The things he used to take for granted had suddenly become far more important to him than clients, success, and money. Then he added, "I don't recommend cancer as an attitude-adjuster, but it will do it for you."

Suffering is a great attitude-adjuster. It can alter our views about what really matters in life.

James says that trouble can teach both the rich and the poor the true values of life (James 1:9-10). Trouble teaches the poor man how rich he is. He learns that he has a wealth of friends. He has a treasure in his church. He has the riches of God's resources. The poor man realizes that he is really a rich man. On the other hand, trouble teaches the rich man just how poor he is. He realizes that material things are not worth much in times of real trouble.

Humility

Third, suffering can make us humble. It knocks a lot of nonsense and arrogance out of us. Suffering teaches us our own weaknesses and that we, like little children, should depend on our heavenly Father for everything. This was the testimony of the Apostle Paul. He faced many hardships as a missionary. He often stared death in the face. Concerning these trials he wrote, "But we had the sentence of death in ourselves, that we should not trust in ourselves, but in God which raiseth the dead" (2 Cor. 1:9).

We've already mentioned Paul's thorn in the flesh. He said that it kept him from being proud, thanks to a special vision he'd had from God (2 Cor. 12:1-10). Here, as in some other passages, we get the impression that humility was not an easy or automatic virture for Paul. But his suffering kept him from pride, so it also kept him useful in the kingdom of God.

Anything that teaches us our own inadequacy and God's sufficiency has value. Even if it is a bad experience, the final result is good.

Repentance

Fourth, suffering can lead us to repentance. It can bring us back to God if we have drifted away. Once while I was preaching at revival meetings, the host pastor took me to visit one of his members. He told me in advance that I would hear a most moving testimony. The man was a radiant Christian who had been blind for over 20 years. Before we left he told me that he had been saved early in his life and for a few years he had walked close to God and had been active in His service. Then he went away from home and away from God. He lived that way for years, until his blindness came. Then, with tears flowing from his eyes, he quoted his favorite Scripture verses: "Before I was afflicted I went astray; but now have I kept Thy Word." And "It is good for me that I have been afflicted; that I might learn Thy statutes" (Ps. 119: 67, 71). His blindness, like the suffering of the psalmist, had brought him to repentance; so he counted it as a blessing.

Faith

Fifth, suffering and the loss of loved ones can give us a greater interest in heaven and the life to come. As troubles and trials weigh heavily on us, we sometimes long for the release and relief of heaven. Losing a loved one in death is like purchasing a piece of real estate in heaven. Now someone is waiting for us there. Our interest in God and the things of eternity become greater than ever before.

Dwight L. Moody said at Henry Drummond's death, "The homegoing of Drummond adds one more attraction to heaven." We often feel the same way.

Robert Service described the experience of many when he wrote:

> I sought Him on the purple seas,
> I sought Him on the peaks aflame;
> Amid the gloom of giant trees
> And canyons lone I called His name;
> The wasted ways of earth I trod:
> In vain! In vain! I found not God
> Then after roamings far and wide,
> In streets and seas and deserts wild,
> I came to stand at last beside
> The deathbed of my little child.
> Lo! As I bent beneath the rod
> I raised my eyes . . . and there was God.
> (*The Complete Poems of Robert Service*, Dodd, Mead.)

Some people never look up until they are flat on their backs. More than one person has found faith in God through suffering and sorrow.

Glorify God

Sixth, suffering can give us an opportunity to glorify God and to witness for Him. Just as the suffering of a young man born blind became an opportunity for Jesus to glorify God (John 9), so our suffering may open new doors for us to glorify Him.

The Apostle Paul actually rejoiced at his imprisonment in Rome because it led to the "furtherance" of the Gospel. The word translated *furtherance* was used to describe woodcutters who preceded an army, cutting a road through the forest, making it possible for the army to advance into regions it could not have gone otherwise. So Paul said his suffering had cut new paths, opened new doors of opportunity for the Gospel. It gave him a chance to preach to his guards (Phil. 1:12-13).

Lucille, a member of my church, fought a long hard bout with cancer. Throughout her suffering she maintained such a radiant, joyful attitude that people marveled at her faith. She used her sickbed as a pulpit from which she witnessed for Christ. Because of the way she responded to her pain and because of what she said, many people were touched and drawn to her Lord. Her suffering gave her a hearing she would not otherwise have had.

Sympathy

Seventh, suffering can make us more sympathetic. It can tenderize our hearts and make us more understanding of others. Those of us who haven't suffered much have a hard time being sympathetic with those who are suffering. Hardships mellow us and make us more compassionate and patient toward others.

Abraham Lincoln was always a greathearted man. But after his son Willie died in February, 1862, his own suffering gave him a tenderness toward others who were suffering. He often visited soldiers' camps, hospitals, and prisons, talking with the men, and winning their confidence and love.

The Apostle Paul said that God comforted him and his co-workers in all their tribulation, so that they might comfort them which were in any trouble, by the comfort which they were comforted by God. (See 2 Cor. 1:4). God used Paul's suffering to equip him to comfort other people.

We are equipped to help others in the same way. In the difficult experiences of life, we learn two things. First, we learn how other people feel and we learn from our own experience that God's grace is adequate. Then we can say to others, "I not only understand how you feel, but when I went through a similar experience, I found God's grace sufficient. And what He did for me He can do for you."

The Bible teaches that we are stewards not only of our possessions, but also of our experiences. We are stewards even of our sorrows and sufferings. God often uses them to equip us to be more effective ministers for Him.

Someone has said, "You can't sharpen an ax on a pound of butter." Sometimes trouble is our whetstone. God uses trouble to sharpen us and make us more effective cutting instruments for Him.

Inspiration

Eighth, our suffering can encourage and inspire the faith of others. Many Christians in the church at Rome had lost their zeal for the Lord. Out of fear of persecution, they had ceased to witness for the Lord. Then the Apostle Paul was imprisoned. When the other Christians saw his courage, cheerfulness, and hope, they were inspired to greater efforts. Many of them began to witness again (Phil. 1:13-18). Many times the faith of one person is made stronger as he sees the faith of another.

Miracles Do Happen

Of course God sometimes chooses to heal those who are suffering and to save the lives of those who are dying in answer to fervent, heartfelt prayer. Miracles can and do happen. While ordinarily God works through medicine, surgery, psychiatry, nursing, and therapy, there are times when He chooses to intervene and to work a miracle. Therefore, no suffering Christian should fail to seek healing from God.

When the Apostle Paul was in prison in Rome, the church at Philippi sent Epaphroditus to deliver a love-offering to Paul and to minister to his needs. While on this mission, Epaphroditus became seriously ill. In fact, Paul said, "He was sick nigh unto death." That word *nigh* literally means "next door neighbor to." Epaphroditus was so sick that he was right next door to death. He was as close to death as he could be without dying. But just at the last moment, God had mercy on him and restored him to health. God healed Epaphroditus not only for his own sake, but also for the sake of the Apostle Paul. If Epaphroditus had died it would have put sorrow on top of the great sorrow which Paul was already experiencing. So, to spare His faithful missionary additional grief, God raised up Epaphroditus (see Phil. 2:27).

The writer of the Book of Kings tells us about King Hezekiah who was on his deathbed when he cried out to God in prayer. God heard his prayers, had mercy on him, and added 15 years to his life (2 Kings 20:1-6). The Apostle Paul himself often stood face-to-face with death, but God delivered him again and again so he could continue his important ministry (2 Cor. 1:9-11; 11:23).

Just a few weeks ago I preached at the funeral of an elderly lady who 13 years ago was given only a few months to live. She had sold her home and moved in with her daughter to live out the last few months of her life. To the amazement of everyone, she lived 13 long years afterward. As long as such unexplained healings happen, we have reason to believe in and ask for miracles.

We therefore ought to heed the admonition of James who wrote, "Is any sick among you? Let him call for the elders of the church; and let them pray over him, anointing him with oil in the name of the Lord; and the prayer of faith shall save the sick, and the Lord shall raise him up" (James 5:14-15).

If you are in the midst of suffering and sorrow, you may not see any good that can come from your experience. But don't despair. It usually takes time for the good aspects of suffering to be seen.

Remember that all things "work together" for our benefit. This means we often can't take isolated events and find good in them. Isolated events in life are like individual ingredients of a cake. Flour, baking soda, and shortening taken separately aren't too tasty. But when mixed together in the right proportions, and cooked at the right temperature for the right length of time, the results can be delicious.

Even so, God can mix all the experiences of our lives—the bad with the good—and bring something worthwhile out of them.

If you keep believing and expecting that, God will not disappoint you. In the meantime, remember that nothing can ever separate you from God's love and care (Rom. 8:35-39).

Part II
How to Die

FOUR

Life
after
All

As never before people are asking, "What's it like to die?" For generations historians, philosophers, and religionists have tried to answer this question. In recent years even scientists have been doing considerable research on it.

That's good, for death is a fact of life. As the German philosopher Martin Heidegger noted, "As soon as a man begins to live, he is old enough to die." We are all engaged to marry Death (see Heb. 9:27); so as we grow older and the ceremony approaches, we need to become better prepared for it.

Even those of us who live in the warmth of the Gospel still feel the chill of death. So we want to know, "What's it like to die?"

The Scriptures remain our best source of information about death and eternity. In their pages we get quite a few glimpses of the mysteries of death and the life beyond.

Biblical writers use four words to describe death. These words can help us understand what it's like for Christians to die.

Sleep

The most common word used to refer to the deaths of Christians in the New Testament is the word *sleep*. It was used 13 times.

The Apostle John used *sleep* once to describe the death of Lazarus. Lazarus was dying. His sisters, Mary and Martha, sent word to Jesus of their brother's illness. They hoped Jesus would come immediately and heal him. But Jesus delayed His journey for several days. Then He told His disciples that He must go and awaken Lazarus, who was asleep.

This puzzled them. They knew that sick people needed rest. Why wake him? They did not understand that Lazarus was dead, so Jesus told them plainly, "Lazarus is dead" (John 11:14).

Luke also used the word *sleep* to describe the death of Stephen. Stephen was stoned to death for preaching the Gospel. As he died he prayed for the forgiveness of those who were killing him. Then Luke wrote, "When he [Stephen] had said this, he fell asleep" (Acts 7:60). The next chapter makes it clear that he died. We read, "Saul was consenting unto his death" and "devout men carried Stephen to his burial" (Acts 8:1-2). In both instances the words *sleep* and *death* were used interchangeably.

Why is the word *sleep* used to describe death? Does it suggest an unconscious existence? By no means! There is no hint in the Bible that at death a person's spirit lapses into a state of unconsciousness. Paul said that for a Christian to be "absent from the body" was to be "present with the Lord" (2 Cor. 5:8). The word *present* means to be "face to face." So at death the earthly bodies of believers begin to decay, but their spirits pass immediately into the presence of God.

An unbeliever, however, goes to Hades at death, where he waits in a conscious state for the resurrection of his body and God's judgment (Luke 16:19-31).

So the word *sleep* does not suggest unconsciousness, but quiet rest. At death God sets His people free from life's toils and cares so that they may enter into the rest of God.

When I was a boy, my dad worked for a railroad. He often spent long hours in the cold and the rain. I can remember him coming home after a hard day's work and sitting down in his easy chair by a warm fire to read the paper while Mom prepared supper. Often as he read he would fall asleep. After a while Mom would call him for dinner and he would awaken refreshed. There was nothing fearful or dreadful about sleeping to Dad. He loved and looked forward to his nap.

Death can be like that for us. Life can be hard. Pressures can mount. Cares can weigh heavily on us. But death brings release and relief from all this. Death is not the end of life. It is like going to sleep at the end of a hard day and awakening refreshed.

Bishop Berggrav of Norway explained death this way: "One day a peasant took his little son on a visit to a village some distance away. On the road, they had to cross a swift stream spanned by a rickety, narrow bridge. It was dark when they started home. The boy remembered the shaky bridge and was frightened.

"His father, noticing his fears, lifted the lad up and carried him in his arms. In a few minutes, the little fellow was fast asleep on his father's shoulder. When he awoke, he was at home with the morning sun streaming through the window of his bedroom."

That's what it's like to die. Dying is going to sleep and awakening at home with our heavenly Father. It is entering into the quiet rest of God.

Depart

Another word used to describe death is *depart* (Phil. 1:23; 2 Tim. 4:6). It means "to unloose, undo, to break up." This word has many applications.

Sometimes the word *depart* referred to unyoking an animal from a plow or a wagon. When the day's work was done, the owner loosed the animal from its burden to rest for the night. Similarly, death for Paul was rest from toil. He would gladly lay his burden down. He was an old man, a veteran of many campaigns, and had earned his honorable discharge. Now he was leaving the work for younger people.

In other cases, the word *depart* described the freeing of a prisoner from chains. Death for Paul was liberation or release. He was in a Roman jail when he penned these words. (See the Epistle to the Philippians.) He felt that death would be exchanging the confines of a Roman prison for the glorious liberties of heaven.

But often the word *depart* referred to loosing the mooring ropes of a ship so it could set sail. The Roman world was alive with travel in Paul's day. Many times he'd been on a ship as it was loosed from the dock and had felt it move into deep water. As a missionary, he stayed on the move. He lived in tents, jails, and homes of friends. But he never forgot his real home. Death to Paul was like boarding a ship, weighing anchor, and sailing home. Rest after toil. Freedom after confinement. A port after a stormy sea.

While writing this paragraph, I am over the Atlantic at the end of a two-week trip to the Bible lands. I have seen many exciting places, including the jail from which Paul wrote these words to the Philippians. It has been the trip of a lifetime. I have stayed in luxurious hotels, eaten delicious food, and enjoyed excellent service. Now I am on my way home.

Although I enjoyed the trip, I never felt completely at ease. I was always a tourist in a foreign land. The language, customs, and values were different. The trip was great, but now I can hardly wait to get home. How good it will be to see my family, sleep in my own bed, and eat at my own table. Home is the greatest place on earth. There's nothing quite like going there after you've been away for a while. That's what it is like for a Christian to die. It's like going home.

Dissolve

The third word used to describe death is *dissolved* (2 Cor. 5:1), or *torn down* (NASB). It means "to fold up a tent and lay it aside." Paul is here comparing our bodies to a tent. A tent is not a permanent dwelling place. It is intended as a temporary home. So are our bodies. They are only the temporary dwelling places of our spirits (our immaterial lives). Our bodies eventually wear out and we have to move out of them.

Paul was a tent-maker by trade. He knew how to make one, put one up, and take one down. So when he thought of his death, he described it as folding up a worn-out tent and laying it aside.

Paul also said that in this body we groan and sigh (2 Cor. 5:2). Ever listen to yourself when you get out of bed in the morning? We all groan and sigh. And the older we get, the more we groan. These groans are evidence that our tents, or bodies are wearing out and beginning to sag.

All of my life I have been athletic. I have played basketball, softball, volleyball, and racketball. At age 45 I am still active. But it's not as easy as it once was. I have more aches and pains than I ever thought possible. Now after I've played hard, I don't sleep well at night. And when I get up in the morning, my groans and moans can be heard throughout the house. I realize that my body is wearing out. One day it will be completely worn out and I will lay it aside in death and move into a new one. Death to Paul was just that. It was moving out of a worn-out, sagging body into a new and better home (Phil. 3:21).

Decease

The fourth word used for death is the word *decease*. It is used once in reference to Jesus' death (Luke 9:31), and once in reference to Peter's death (2 Peter 1:13-15).

The word means "an exodus" or "a going out." It is rooted in Old Testament history. One of the greatest events in Jewish history, the Exodus, was the time when Moses led the Children of Israel out of slavery in Egypt and up to the Promised Land of God.

When Peter thought of his own death, he thought of it as going to the Promised Land of God. It was "a way out" from the old gloom into a new glory. Death for the children of God is an accomplishment. Like the Children of Israel in Egypt, we are pursued by relentless foes: the world, the flesh, and the devil. Weakness, sickness, old age—all pursue us. We are always "strangers and pilgrims" here on earth (1 Peter 2:11). One day we too will move up to God's Promised Land.

We think we're in the land of the living on our way to the land of dying. The opposite is true. We Christians are really in the land of the dying on our way to the land of the living.

For us Christians, death is not the end, but a step to becoming. It is not ceasing to be, but putting out the lamp because the dawn has come. We are on our way out!

The last words of Missionary James Barnes were, "I have been dying for 20 years; now I am going to live."

So, what is it like for a Christian to die? It's like going to sleep and waking up refreshed. It's like weighing anchor and sailing for home. It's like laying aside a worn-out tent and moving into a permanent home. It's like going to the Promised Land of God.

That's why Paul could write of himself, "For to me to live is Christ, and to die is gain. . . . For I am in a strait betwixt two, having a desire to depart, and to be with Christ; which is far better" (Phil. 1:21-23).

These were not the words of a bitter old man who was fed up with life and wanted to die. He was not saying death was the lesser of two evils. He was saying that it was the greater of two blessings. To Paul life was good. But to depart and be with Christ was much better. He considered it a net gain. So should every Christian.

All available evidence converges at this point. Life does not end at the cemetery. There is life beyond and we enter it through the death experience. And for us as Christians, it is a life of joy, peace, wholeness, and reunion, which God has prepared for us.

FIVE

Am
I
Normal?

Ann came to see me at the insistence of a friend. Several months earlier her husband of over 20 years had died and she was having a hard time handling her grief. She was actually worried about her emotional stability.

She said, "I find myself immobile at times. I sometimes go for days without doing anything around the house. I'm cross and irritable with my children. It's just not like me! I'm not myself!

"I know I ought to be in church, but I can't make myself go. Last Sunday I just sat home, looked out the window, and cried all day. Sometimes I feel like my insides could break in two."

Then she asked, "Am I normal? Is something wrong with me? Am I about to have a nervous breakdown?"

I assured Ann that she was perfectly normal. A part of her problem was that she had never been through grief like this before, so she didn't understand what was happening to her. Few of us do at such times. When death comes, scores of emotions flood into our lives uninvited. Although most of us have experienced anxiety, depression, bitterness, and self-pity at various times and in varying degrees; now suddenly they push, shove, and elbow their way into our lives all at once in overwhelming degrees. Like Ann, each of us wonders, "Am I normal? Am I losing my mind? Is something wrong with me?'' Our problem is that no one ever told us what to expect in the grieving process.

We need to be forewarned about some of the emotions that usually accompany grief so that we can understand what is happening to us. Here are some of these emotions:

Shock

The first emotion that usually follows the death of a loved one is shock. We simply cannot believe what has happened. It seems like a dream and we keep expecting to wake up and find out that it is not true. Grief often has the effect of an anesthetic on us. It leaves us numb, bewildered, and confused. The numbness is normal and is actually a blessing. It is like an internal, emotional shock absorber that helps you take the stunning blows of life. We sometimes refer to the loss of a loved one as ''a blow.'' That's exactly what it is. It's an emotional blow that actually dazes or paralyzes us into inaction and indecision so that for a while our reactions are not normal.

This shock may remain for some time. Grief relieves itself eventually, but it takes its own course, and sometimes the course is slow and difficult. Someone has called the separation caused by death an emotional amputation. I am told that amputees often feel strong sensations in the parts of their bodies that are no longer there. The nerve system of the leg may be gone, but the nerve connections in the brain are still able to ''feel'' pains in the limb. In time, that part of the brain adapts itself to the absence of the leg. Then the sensation ceases. But this does not occur at once; it is a slow process, set to nature's deliberate time schedule.

In the same way, it is impossible to accept the death of a loved one quickly. Gradually, the knowledge of what has happened will seep into every corner of your mind, and you will be able to realistically cope with the fact that your loved one is dead.

In James Fennimore Cooper's *The Last of the Mohicans*, the Indian chief's only son is killed while trying to save the life of the colonel's daughter. After the funeral the girl asks Hawkeye, ''What will the chief do?''

Hawkeye replied, "It takes the Mohican only a few minutes to bury the dead. It takes him months to bury his grief" (Dodd, Mead). We are the same way.

Anxiety

Following close behind shock is anxiety or fear. This was the immediate reaction of the disciples when Jesus told them of His approaching death. They could not believe it. For three years He had been the center of their lives. They had walked with Him, learned from Him, and depended on Him. They had forsaken all to follow Him. Now they would be left alone. What would they do without Him? Naturally they were distressed (John 14:1).

If you have depended heavily on the person who died for financial or emotional support, you probably feel that the whole foundation of your life has crumbled and you feel lost and alone. This is always frightening. You may wonder, "What am I going to do now? How am I going to live? Who will take care of me?" You may even panic. You may dread tomorrow and the next day and the day after.

Last year my father died. Before and after the funeral, a large number of friends and family members came to our house. A few hours after the funeral, all the friends were gone. A few days later, all the family except me was gone. As I was preparing to return to my home, Mother told me that this would be the first night she had spent alone in over 50 years. That would be frightening for anyone.

Anxiety is a normal emotion when the established foundations of life are shattered. In time we may find support from our family, friends, and our faith, and this feeling will ease, but at first it is almost overwhelming.

Depression

Depression is that midnight of the soul that settles on us when we lose someone we love. How could it be otherwise?

Oftentimes a wife's whole life revolves around her family. She prepares their meals, washes their clothes, gets them to school and to work on time, and listens to their troubles. She may not have much in life apart from them.

When death comes to one of them, she may wonder how she can go on living, or even if she wants to. A big reason for living has passed. A sense of futility and loneliness may follow.

C.S. Lewis, in *A Grief Observed* (Seabury), said concerning the loss of his wife, "Her absence is like the sky, spread over everything." We too find ourselves sitting day after day, staring out into space with a sense of futility and emptiness. We may feel fatigued, restless, unable to concentrate. We may try to put those thoughts of our loved one out of our minds, but we find that they keep coming back as the tide keeps coming back to the shore. We may pray and feel that the heavens are empty. We may wonder if the sun will ever shine again.

King David, during the fatal illness of a little son, experienced depression. He would not eat and he could not sleep. He neglected his appearance and health. In fact he was so distraught that his servants were afraid he might harm himself (2 Sam. 12:16-18). We may feel the same way.

Depression and despair are to be expected. These feelings may linger over us like a heavy fog for many months. But one day they will pass and one day we will again experience the sunshine of life and hope and joy again.

Regret

I spoke recently with a young man whose father had just died of a heart attack. I asked him how his mother was doing. He said, "She's feeling guilty. Dad said he felt bad this morning and she wishes she had taken him to the doctor right then."

That kind of guilt and regret often fills our minds after a loved one dies. We remember things we might have done or not done, words which we might have said or wish we could retract. We are apt to say such things as:

"Oh, if I had only done more for him while he was alive."

Or, "If I had been more concerned and sensitive to his needs . . ."

Or "If I had only called the doctor sooner . . ."

Or "I wish I could tell her again that I'm sorry and that I really love her."

Or "I wish I had never said that."

Or "I wish I had not let her go on that trip."

Almost everyone experiences some feelings like these.

Vance Havner, speaking about the death of his wife of 33 years, gave some good advice about regrets. He said, "Don't wear yourself out saying, 'If I had only, if only I had thought of this before my troubles came, before my loved one went. If only I had done this, if only, if only, if only.' Turn your back on that. You can drive yourself crazy in the world of 'if I had only.' I'm still walking through the valley, but thank God I'm walking through it, not wallowing in it. There is a big difference."

Self-Pity

When death comes to someone close, we are apt to cry out, "Why me? Why me?" or "It's not fair."

These are cries of self-pity. For when those we love who are Christians die, our grief and sorrow is really for ourselves. Our loved ones are now beyond suffering and pain. They have gone to a far better life. Our grief then is really self-grief. We weep for ourselves. We are weeping because of our own loss and loneliness, not theirs.

Some self-pity is normal. There is a tinge of it in all of us. However, we must not give in to it. A pastor was visited by some friends shortly after his wife died. He was 86 years old at the time. He had suffered a nervous breakdown early in his ministry and had spent several months in a sanitarium. The friends expected to find him shattered by the loss of the wife he had cherished for more than 60 years. Instead, he met them with a smile.

He said, "Florence enjoyed good health, you know, right to the end. I'm the one who had ailments, and I was afraid I'd die first and leave her alone. Now she's gone, and I will be the one to face loneliness. I'm so thankful for that. This is something I can do for Florence."

Bitterness

Bitterness, resentment, and anger may also often accompany the loss of a loved one. These feelings may be directed at almost anyone. They may be directed at other members of the family if it is felt that they did not do their part in caring for the deceased. It usually falls to one person in the family to care for parents when they are old or sick. Sometimes this person becomes bitter because he feels that the other members of the family took advantage of him.

Bitterness may be directed at the attending physician. We may feel that he could have come sooner or could have done more to save our loved one. We often expect our doctors to be miracle-workers. They aren't. Many times they bear the brunt of bitterness they do not deserve.

Bitterness may even be directed at God. We may feel that He has let us down. I used to feel that I had to defend Him against all such attacks. I don't anymore. I now realize that such outbursts are really signs of faith. People don't get angry at someone they don't believe in.

At times we may be bitter without being down on any one person in particular. A young mother who lost a two-year-old son in a drowning accident said she often felt resentment when she saw other mothers with their children. She said, "I'm ashamed to admit it now, but I used to wonder why they should have their children when I couldn't have mine."

Beware of bitterness. It is like a bag of stones carried on your shoulder and never set down. It becomes heavier with the passing of the years. As your strength lessens, eventually the bag becomes so heavy that you stagger under its weight. It is sad to see you bent double by a back-breaking burden you don't have to carry.

There is a better way to deal with sorrow. Darrell and Doris taught me this a few years ago. Their only son, a junior college student, was shot in an unexplained murder. They were both devout Christians, but this rocked them on their heels. How could they bear not knowing why he was shot, or who did it?

Naturally, they fought feelings of anger, hatred, and bitterness.

A few days after the funeral, I received a letter from them. The following is excerpted from it:

> We are overwhelmed with the peace God has given to us. We don't deserve it. We didn't even have to ask for it. It was just a gift. I guess our part was accepting it (just like salvation). And this accepting meant giving Terry up completely, with no hostility toward God for "letting this happen to us."
>
> We don't get any comfort trying to understand or figure out why it happened. Terry is gone. Nothing will bring him back. Our comfort comes from God.
>
> You were right. God *does* have laws. Sparrows *do* fall. We have hit bottom but we have found it solid. . . .

Mixed Emotions

Sometimes death may actually be a welcome relief. When the illness has been prolonged and there has been intense pain, our family may become physically and emotionally drained. We may feel a sense of thanksgiving that it is all over. That's understandable.

However, if we aren't careful, we may feel guilty about being thankful that the person has died. We may feel that we shouldn't feel thankful.

All these emotions—bitterness, guilt, resentment, self-pity, and the like—can grow together in your life as a result of sorrow and grief. Understand that they are normal. Expect them to visit you.

But don't make these emotions your lifelong friends. Face them, deal with them, and in time bid them good-bye and get on with the responsibilities and joys of living. That's the way to deal with them.

SIX

Broken Hearts Do Heal

The death of a loved one is about the most shattering experience that can befall us. It is as if the light of life has gone out, and we are left to wonder in the darkness alone. Grief is a destructive force, violent in its attack and grim in its persistency. If we aren't liberated from grief in a reasonable period of time, we shall be overcome by it.

Many feel that when grief comes, there is not much that can be done about it. It can only be endured. This is not so. We must handle grief or it will handle us. We are not meant to sit and brood or give in to grief. While no words or theory or formula can deaden the immediate overwhelming pain of bereavement, we can do some things to lessen grief's blow. Here are seven suggestions to help us handle and overcome our grief:

Turn to God

First, ask God to help you. This is the most meaningful thing you can do to handle grief. Paul calls God "the God of all comfort" (2 Cor. 1:3). The Latin word for *comfort* is "fortus." It means to "fortify."

God can fortify, strengthen, and sustain us in our suffering. He does not exempt us from troubles, but He will sustain us while we are having them, if we turn to Him. This has been the testimony of God's people throughout the ages.

Three years ago one of my sisters was diagnosed as having lung cancer. Within a week she died. She had been born deaf and had never learned to talk. She had never married and so lived all of her 50 years with my parents. This made her death extra hard on them. I was on a mission trip in Brazil at the time and could not be reached. It was two weeks before I learned of her death.

My mother has always been very emotional, and I feared that she might have been overcome by grief at the funeral service. When I arrived back in the States, I immediately went to see my parents. As we talked about the service, I asked Mom how she coped at the funeral. I really expected her to say how difficult it was. But she didn't. She said, "I did fine. I just asked God to strengthen me, and He did." It was as simple, or as profound, as that. Though I have been preaching that truth for over 25 years, I was still surprised at her answer. It reminded me again of just how ready and able God is to help us, if we turn to Him.

Fritz and Shirley are another example of how the Lord strengthens in sorrow. Fritz is a popular evangelistic singer; Shirley is his wife and accompanist. Greta, their lovely and vivacious daughter, was killed in a head-on automobile collision just two weeks after she graduated from high school.

A thousand people attended her funeral service, which was characterized by hope and victory in Jesus. As I closed the service at the graveside, Fritz began to sing softly, "Alleluia." In a moment everyone around the grave had joined him in singing this beautiful song of faith.

Several months later Fritz shared his testimony about how God had sustained him in his grief. He said, "People often tell me, 'I don't believe I could stand to go through an experience like that.' " Then he added, "On June 15th, I couldn't have stood it either. But on June 16th, the day Greta died, I had God's grace and strength to help me."

In the same way God's grace is available to you—just when you need it, if you'll only ask for it. Through prayer, Bible study, and worship you can find that inner strength to help you handle your grief.

Accept Death as a Part of Life

Second, accept death as a part of life. Death is as much a part of life as birth and growth. Unbeliever George Bernard Shaw was right when he said, "Life's ultimate statistic is the same for all—one out of one dies."

Though the average life span increases a little every year, no one has a guarantee of tomorrow, and we know that death is inevitable. With the passing years, our physical bodies wear out. Accidents and diseases continue to claim their victims and always will. The last enemy of man to be defeated will be death. So death should be anticipated. We must accept it as a part of life.

Express Your Grief

Third, express your grief through tears. Sue had just gone through her first holiday season since her husband died. Holidays, birthdays, and anniversaries were especially hard for her. She often found herself unable to hold back unexplained tears. She said, "I worry about myself, crying this way. Shouldn't I be over this by now?"

I tried to assure her that tears were a normal part of the healing process, and that she should not be ashamed of them, or worried because of them.

Tears are one of nature's safety valves. Crying depressurizes us emotionally, and thus relieves stresses that may affect even our bodies. We are much like pressure cookers. There must be a release valve or an emotional explosion may take place. So, we shouldn't bear our sorrows. Instead, we need to release them.

But some person may say, "You've got to keep your chin up. You've got to be brave. Tears are a denial of your faith."

We shouldn't believe that. Tears are a natural expression of the emotion of grief. Jesus Himself wept beside the grave of his friend Lazarus. And we are told to "weep with them that weep" (Rom.

12:15). Paul says, "I wrote unto you with many tears" (2 Cor. 2:4). The same God who gave us lips to smile with also gave us tear ducts to cry with. One is as natural as the other.

We are told not to sorrow as if we have no hope (1 Thes. 4:13–18). But this doesn't forbid sorrow. Hope will limit sorrow. Total abstinence from sorrow would be impossible but moderation is desirable.

So fighting back the tears doesn't fool anybody, or solve anything, or even reveal a strong expression of faith. Emotions require actions. Love requires the expression of affection. And sorrow usually requires some tears.

So remember that periods of sobbing will come. Don't be ashamed of them. They are part of the healing process.

Live through Your Memories

Fourth, take time to live through your memories of your loved one. Don't try to run away from these experiences. Don't hide their reality in the dark closet of your mind, trying to forget them.

Some well-meaning person may tell you, "You need a long trip. You need to get away from it all." But that's not true. The best place to face readjustment is where the readjustment must be finally made—at home. There will be a time for rest, a change, a trip later. But running away from your memories is not the answer.

It is most probable that you need to look at pictures from the past, listen to familiar music you both loved, walk down familiar paths and visit beloved shops, look at favorite chairs, toys, books, or clothes, and talk with friends with whom the deceased was close. Live with the memories; don't run from them. Recovering from grief never means a total erasure of all memories of the deceased. This cannot be done.

What to do with possessions of a loved one presents a special problem. The life of the person is so associated with them that even the handling of them may bring tears. When Dorcas died, her friends wept as they viewed the garments she had made for them (Acts 9:39). We may do the same thing.

Some people want nothing to do with their loved one's possessions. They prefer that someone else clears out the closets and removes all remembrances. Others cling to every possession as though they expect the loved one to come back at any time. Neither approach is healthy or healing. Both are, in a sense, a denial of the reality of death.

So don't get someone else to clean up your loved one's room. Do it yourself. It will be hard, but it will help heal your broken heart faster.

You will want to move slowly when making important decisions that cannot be reversed. Time gives perspective and the passing of days makes it possible to see more clearly what is important and what is not. Many people have regretted hurried decisions such as selling the house and moving in with someone else.

So, living through the memories will help heal your memories.

Talk Out Your Grief

Fifth, talk out your grief. Sorrow needs not only to be expressed in tears, but also in words. A part of the secret of psychotherapy is that we rid ourselves of pent-up emotions by verbalizing them. Talking gives relief and release to feelings of grief, as well as to feelings of bitterness, resentment, and anger. Find someone to talk with. It may be a friend or relative or the pastor of your church. The person does not have to be a professional counselor.

Choose someone who is interested in you and who will take the time to listen. Select someone who will not be shocked, who will keep confidences, and who has a strong faith in you, and in God. Find that person and pour out your heart to him or her.

An outstanding psychiatrist once said, ''More psychotherapy is accomplished between two good friends at coffee at 10 A.M. than all day long in the doctor's office. A good talk with a close friend can solve problems or at least put them in perspective before they become overpowering.''

Stay Busy

Sixth, find work to do. In time tears will cease to flow as rapidly and as abundantly as they once did. You will have lived through some of your memories. You will have talked with other people about your sorrow. Now you will need to get involved in some kind of work.

During his child's critical illness, King David isolated himself in grief. He wept and fasted and prayed. But when the child died, he went first to worship God and then plunged back into his heavy responsibilities as the leader of his people (2 Sam. 12:20). This was the best thing he could do.

Somebody said, "Grief thrives in the soil of idleness." Without question this is true. Bereavement can be eased some by keeping busy. We are fortunate if we have work to be done, duties to be performed, necessities which command attention. We need to keep in touch with many practical things which simply have to be taken care of.

But don't rush back to work too soon. That doesn't solve the problem and may repress it. Though work may often serve as a legitimate antidote for yourself, work may also become a means of denying grief. But don't wait too long either. You can spend all of your energy and efforts drowning in self-pity, or you can direct your sorrow toward some meaningful end. Nothing helps like getting to work at something creative and unique. Life is like riding a bicycle. It is difficult to keep your balance while standing still, but when moving forward it's easier to maintain your balance. Creative work will help to divert your mind for increasing periods of time.

Think of Life as a Gift

Seventh, think of life as a gift. Human beings do not own one another. We are God's children. We belong to Him. It is only by grace that we are together for a time, for a little while. We should receive God's gift of other people in our lives with thanksgiving. But we must realize that people are gifts—we cannot hang on or refuse to let go of God's children when He calls them.

John Powell observed once that Jesus used two images in His parables to describe the coming of death. One was "a thief in the night" and the other was "a bridegroom coming to claim his beloved.'' ''The difference,'' said Powell, ''was not in the nature of death, but in the attitude of the individual toward what he had. For example, to those who attached themselves possessively to another and claimed that person by right, death seemed like a thief. But to those who realized that all things belong to God and are ours by grace, death is deemed as Original Love calling its own. Here is another insight of biblical revelation that enables us to see death in a holy, new perspective. It is not a thief, though it may well appear that way to young eyes. It is really life's gracious Host knocking gently at our door to reclaim that which is actually His own'' (*A Reason to Live, a Reason to Die*, Argus Communications).

Grief Can Be Handled

If you have recently lost a loved one, you may feel you will never recover, but you will if you handle it correctly. In chapter 2 I told you about Eloise Hammack who had cancer. She died after a long illness. A year later her husband sent me a letter that is a marvelous testimony about how to handle grief. It was addressed to his two married daughters. He sent a copy to me because of our close friendship.

Dear Elaine and Carolyn:

October 22 marks a year since Eloise went to heaven. While I have stayed busy, I have had much time to think and remember, especially at night and on weekends. With the passing of a year, I am much better able to cope with the problem and have obtained a degree of serenity.

My loss was the most humbling experience of my life. It put me on my knees, so to speak, with no place to look except up. But I found that time is a great healer. Losing Eloise was somewhat like losing a right arm. It hurts so much at first, then healing starts and the pain diminishes, but every time you look down you are reminded of your loss.

I have worked hard at several things which explains my progress. Counting my blessings has been such a big help. Here are some of them: a storehouse of fond memories of our

44-year partnership, a minimum number of regrets. Reasonably good health—and I really don't feel my age! A zest for living and a sense of humor. Enough of this world's goods not to be worried about money matters. My physical and mental ability to work, play golf, and enjoy friends. Opportunities to brighten the lives of others. My appreciation of life itself. A long list of answered prayers. Two lovely daughters and their families who I know love me very much. A firm and seasoned faith in God and a renewed assurance of a future life in heaven. Considering all the good things, I would be most ungrateful if I complained now.

I have learned some truths in a deeper sense this past year: (1) "To everything there is a season and a time to every purpose . . . a time to be born and a time to die" (Ecc. 3:1–2). (2) Friends mean more than ever before in stressful times. They are, indeed, the spice of life. (3) God is truly great. The song "How Great Thou Art" has more significance to me now. (4) I believe I have learned something of the real meaning of the "presence of the Holy Spirit." His Spirit has ministered so closely to me at home that it is almost like having conversations with a good friend. I now know better about what the columnist meant when he referred to the "brush of angel's wings." No, I am not a saint and I hope I haven't lost my marbles! I am the same guy you have always known but have just been brought closer to God.

I hope you will not consider this letter an expression of self-pity, but that it will strengthen, not sadden, you. I am writing you for two reasons: to release thoughts that have occurred to me often (a selfish reason) and to possibly help you in your everyday life, realizing that you too had a great loss on October 22.

Love,
Your Dad

You see, grief can be handled. Broken hearts do heal. "How long will the pain of grief last?" you ask. As long as you live. You never quite forget, no matter how many years pass. The loss of a loved one is like a major operation; a part of you is removed and you have the scar the rest of your life.

This does not mean that the pain continues with the same intensity. There is a short while, at first, when the wound is very painful. Then it begins to heal. But a scar will always remain.

Still, remember that it is not only the pain which will last, but also the blessed memories. So focus on them and keep going.

Part III

How to Help

SEVEN

How to Help a Grieving Friend

A few days before Christmas, I visited with a couple whose 13-year-old boy had accidentally shot himself to death. Though his parents had made great progress in overcoming their grief, I knew that the holiday season would be especially hard on them. Holidays always seem to intensify grief. So I dropped by just to spend a few minutes with them. As we talked about their loss, the mother said, "There was a time when we actually wondered if we would ever laugh again."

Grief is one of the most exacting of all the emotions of life. When death takes someone we love—a sister, a brother, a husband, a wife, a mother, a father, or a friend, it is often as if the light of our life has gone out. Our whole world is blackened and saddened by our great loss. We too may wonder if we will ever laugh again.

Friends can play a vital part in overcoming grief. Life is not meant to be lived as a solo but as a chorus. That's why biblical writers often speak of our responsibilities to help one another in the hard times of life. Paul wrote, "Bear ye one another's burdens, and so fulfill the law of Christ" (Gal. 6:2). "We then that are strong ought to bear the infirmities of the weak" (Rom. 15:1).

63

"Rejoice with them that do rejoice, and weep with them that weep" (Rom. 12:15).

In times of darkness after a great loss, a friend can bring some light by his presence, concern, and sympathy. Fewer crises in life afford friends an opportunity for more genuine ministry than does a time of grief.

It was a part of the life and ministry of Jesus to "heal the brokenhearted" (Luke 4:18). The Apostle John gives us an example of how Jesus went about this ministry as he tells us of Jesus' visits with Mary and Martha after the death of their brother Lazarus (John 11:1-45). The ministry of Jesus to these friends in grief becomes a pattern for us. His example helps us see how we can minister to our grieving friends.

Jesus was on a preaching mission when word came to Him that Lazarus was critically ill. By the time He arrived at the town of Bethany, Lazarus had already died and had been buried for four days. When Martha heard that Jesus was coming, she ran to meet Him and said to Him:

> "Lord, if You had been here, my brother would not have died. Even now I know that whatever You ask of God, God will give You."
> Jesus said to her, "Your brother shall rise again."
> Martha said to Him, "I know that he will rise again in the resurrection on the last day."
> Jesus said to her, "I am the Resurrection and the Life; he who believes in Me shall live even if he dies, and everyone who lives and believes in Me shall never die" (John 11:21-26, NASB).

Martha rushed home to tell her sister Mary that Jesus had come. So Mary went to meet Him also. When she reached Jesus, she was in deep sorrow and fell down at Jesus' feet, saying that if He had been there her brother would not have died.

When Jesus saw her and their friends weeping, He was greatly distressed. Then the Apostle John states simply, "Jesus wept."

Those who observed Jesus weeping said, "Behold how He loved him!" (See John 11:35-36.)

Jesus asked to be taken to the grave of Lazarus and commanded the stone to be rolled back from the entrance of the cave where Lazarus had been buried. Then He shouted, "Lazarus, come forth!"

To the amazement of all, Lazarus was awakened from the sleep of death and came out of the tomb alive. As a result of this mighty miracle, many of the friends of Mary and Martha were convinced that Jesus was the Son of God.

In this experience we have an example of how Jesus ministered to His grieving friends. He did four things to help them in their sorrow:

1. Jesus went (John 11:17).
2. Jesus wept (11:35).
3. Jesus witnessed (11:23-26).
4. Jesus woke Lazarus (11:43-44).

The ministry of Jesus to these grieving friends shows us how we can help our grieving friends also.

Make Yourself Available to Your Grieving Friend

The first thing Jesus did on hearing of Lazarus' death was to go to be with the family. That's the first thing we ought to do also.

"But," you tell me, "I feel so inadequate. I don't know what to say." Don't let that stop you. We all feel helpless at a time like that. I have been visiting people in their grief for 25 years and I still feel inadequate.

It helped me when I finally realized that I do not need to say anything at all. Why do we feel we must say something to give immediate relief to those under stress? What our grieving friends need is not an instant sermon, nor a simple answer, nor a long Scripture quotation. What they need is our concern. Our personal presence means more than any words we might say.

Besides, I have learned through the years that answers do not heal broken hearts. Explanations do not soothe troubled spirits. Only God, friends, and time can do that.

Once a young couple lost their only child, a beautiful three-year-old daughter, as a result of a freak accident. Unable to justify this tragedy with their concept of a loving God, they went to their minister for help.

"Why?" they asked.

"It was God's will," the minister told them.

The couple couldn't accept that answer and sought out the assistant pastor. He quoted yards of Scripture, trying to give them comfort, but his many words fell on deaf ears.

Finally, they turned to a dear elderly woman in the church. She had little formal education, but she knew her Bible well. Surely she could give them a spiritual answer. After hearing the details of the child's death, the old saint didn't utter a single word. Instead she tenderly wrapped her arms around the heartbroken couple's shoulders. Together they cried some of the hurt away.

Sometimes when answers aren't easy, your best statement is silent caring and a tender touch. Even God does not promise you answers for all the sorrows of life. He only promises to be with you. There is no more powerful way to communicate caring than by your presence and your touch. So go to them. Give them a warm handclasp, a loving pat on the shoulder, or a tender embrace. That will say all that needs to be said.

Don't worry about words. Just make yourself available to your bereaved friends. Being there is enough. Often, what your friend needs most is an understanding and sympathetic listener. When Ezekiel went to minister to the exiles, he began by sitting among them for seven days, saying nothing but just listening. That might be the best place for you to begin also. Allow the grieving friend an opportunity to talk and take time to listen. Talking out his grief or speaking about the mixed feelings which he has about the deceased provides the bereaved person an occasion to release bottled-up emotions. Being a good listener is more important than being a good talker in helping a grieving friend.

Don't ask the bereaved person if there is anything you can do; either ask another relative or simply look around and see what needs to be done. Someone must answer the telephone; someone needs to greet friends at the door; someone needs to care for small children if there are any; someone needs to do the washing, ironing, and cooking. Just do what needs to be done. But the most important thing of all is to be there. So when you learn that a friend has had a death in the family, go to be with him. That's what Jesus did. Jesus went.

Help Your Grieving Friend Express His Emotions

A second thing Jesus did in ministering to Mary and Martha was to weep with them. The verse "Jesus wept" (11:35) is the shortest verse in the Bible. However, it speaks volumes about Jesus and how He helped His grieving friends. It suggests to us that Jesus entered into the experience of grief with Mary and Martha. He felt what they felt. He shared their deep sorrow. He wept and He allowed them to weep also.

To help a friend in grief, you need to be the kind of person with whom the griever can weep unashamedly, knowing that you are suffering with him.

Many times we, as friends, will mistakenly say: "Oh, don't cry; it will be all right." Our society has put a taboo on such external signs of emotion. Tears are often viewed as an evidence of weakness, or of one's inability to deal with the situation. Some even consider tears a sign of a lack of faith; any outward display of emotion is taken to be unmanly or unchristian.

The stoic attitude is usually the one that receives the greatest praise from well-meaning friends: "Oh, you're being so brave." "You are taking it so well." "How wonderful you are, not letting this throw you."

Instead of such unreal pretense in the light of one's loss, we need to encourage the right of the grief sufferer to mourn. "Grief," as Edgar Jackson has observed, "is an honorable emotion."

People need to weep. Tears are an avenue of expression which God has given us to release the pent-up emotions which if kept inside might distort our personality with the power of their internal agitations.

Several years ago I visited a home where a lady had attempted suicide a few hours earlier by taking a bottle of aspirin. Members of her family were forcing her to drink cups and cups of hot coffee when we arrived.

The lady asked if she could talk with me privately. Then she told me that a year before, her son had been burned almost to death. His condition had required several skin grafts and months and months of hospitalization. During all of that emotional strain she said, "My husband kept saying, 'Don't cry! Don't cry!' " Then she revealed the root of much of her problem when she said, "A mother wants to cry over her children. I've had this all bottled up in me too long."

A little girl lost a playmate in death, and one day reported to her family that she had gone to comfort the sorrowing mother. "What did you tell her?" the father asked.

"Nothing," the child replied, "I just climbed up on her lap and cried with her."

Probably no one ministered to that mother more than the little child who shared in her deep grief. Remember that Jesus said, "Blessed are they that mourn; for they shall be comforted" (Matt. 5:4). And remember that Jesus Himself wept. We need to do the same.

Give Your Grieving Friend Assurance and Hope

The third thing Jesus did was to witness to Martha. He gave her assurance and hope for the future. He assured her that her brother would live again. After she said she believed Lazarus would live again in the last days, Jesus said an amazing thing. He told her, "I am the Resurrection, and the Life. He that believeth in Me, though he were dead, yet shall he live." Jesus was saying that the resurrection was not just some far-off event. He Himself was the Resurrection. He was its source, its power, its reality. He was saying, "The Resurrection is in your midst right now." What a comfort and encouragement this had to be to Martha.

We too must affirm the reality of the Resurrection along with God's love and presence to our grieving friends. It is not enough just to share our friends' sorrow. We should also try to share our Saviour. When the time seems right we must try to lift them into God's presence. We must bring them into contact with the spiritual resources that can sustain and strengthen them in their time of great loss. We must point them beyond the despair of that moment to the hope that Jesus Christ offers.

The best witness we can give, of course, grows out of our own experiences. Richard Baxter, (Christian author of books on death) who was criticized by a friend for grieving too long over the death of his wife, declared, "I will not be judged by those who have never known the like." Those who have felt the pangs of sorrow can reach out a sympathetic hand of understanding because they have felt as their friends have felt. They have ached. They have cried. They have walked the dark valley of grief before, and now they can extend a hand.

However, you need not have endured every experience to share the truth of God with others in a meaningful way. The Word of God has power in itself and it will strengthen people, even if you have never been through what they are going through.

You are a steward of all of your experiences of life, including sorrow. So be a witness to others about God's sustaining grace. When the time seems right, tell your friends what God has done for you and what He can do for them. Jesus witnessed and so should you.

How to Help a Non-Christian Friend

What if your grieving friend is not a Christian? Or if he is a Christian but the person who has died was not a Christian? All of us face this from time to time.

Even if your grieving friend is not a Christian, there is a word of comfort and hope you can give him. You can assure him of God's love and care for him and urge him to turn to the Lord for strength to face his sorrow. Your grieving friend may be more sensitive to spiritual things at this time than ever before. The loss of his loved one may have made him aware of his need for Christ and thus more receptive to His help.

Peter tells us to cast all our cares upon the Lord because He cares for us (1 Peter 5:7). The word *cast* means "to throw upon." It is the same word that was used to describe the disciples throwing their garments on the colt that Jesus used for His triumphant entry into Jerusalem (Luke 19:35). In the same way that they cast their garments on the colt, we are told to cast all our cares on the Lord.

The basis for our casting is His caring. That is an amazing fact. Think about it for a moment. The great God of the universe cares about us! Light travels at the speed of 186,000 miles per second. If we could leave the earth traveling that fast, in two seconds we would pass the moon. In eight and one-half minutes we would pass the sun. Five hours later we would be out of our solar system. Four years later we would zip by the nearest star. One million, five-hundred thousand years after that, we would come to the most distant galaxy we know about.

How much further could we travel? After four and one-half million years, traveling at the speed of light, we would reach that area of the universe that cannot be seen by telescope from this planet. Who knows what lies beyond that? Now, we need to remember that the Creator of all of this says, "I care for you."

The psalmist tells us that if we will cast our burdens on the Lord, He will sustain us (Ps. 55:22). The word *sustain* means "to strengthen or support." That's what the Lord promises to do for us if we turn to Him. He will strengthen and support us in our sorrow. He will keep us on our feet in the midst of the storm of life.

Jesus Himself gives all of us a great invitation to come to Him for help when He says, "Come unto Me, all ye that labor and are heavy laden, and I will give you rest. Take My yoke upon you, and learn of Me; for I am meek and lowly in heart, and ye shall find rest unto your souls" (Matt. 11:28-29). We can share these marvelous promises and invitations with all our friends, whether they are Christians or not.

But what if the person who has died was not a Christian? Is there any word of comfort we can give to his grieving family? How can we help them in their time of sorrow? Last week I received a phone call from a lady whose father-in-law was critically ill. Her husband had serious doubts about his father's Christian commitment and was wondering about his father's eternal destiny. She told me that her husband just couldn't believe that God would send his dad to hell.

We know, of course, that God does not send people to hell. Sin does. If people are lost, it is because they choose to be. We know also that when unbelievers die all hope is gone (Prov. 11:7). However, we do not need to emphasize these things to our grieving friends. I said to her, "Fortunately, we do not have to make judgments about other people. That's God's business. We never know for sure what is in a person's heart. He might come to faith in Christ in his last days or even the last hours of his life and no one will know about it. The thief on the cross turned in faith to Jesus at the last possible moment. Your father-in-law may do the same thing. Hang on to that hope and remember that fortunately we do not have to and should not attempt to pass judgment on others."

One thing we can be sure of is that God will deal fairly with all people. Abraham asked, "Shall not the Judge of all the earth do right?" (Gen. 18:25) The unanimous testimony of Scripture is, "Yes. Emphatically so." No person will ever be able to look God in the face and say, "You were not fair with me." God will be absolutely just with everyone in eternity. So we must always trust our loved ones to the love, mercy, and fairness of God.

Help Your Grieving Friend Find a New Vision of Life

The fourth thing Jesus did was to awaken Lazarus from the dead. We of course cannot do this. But we can awaken our grieving friends to new hope, new life, and to new usefulness. A grieving friend often feels that a part of himself has died and been forever buried in the grave. He may feel there is nothing left to live for. He may see no reason to go on. But he must. And you, as a friend, may be able to help direct him into a renewed vision of life and into meaningful service.

Your friend's grief can cause him to turn inward and long for pity, or to turn outward and search for ways to help others. Many have lost sons or daughters, husbands or wives, mothers or fathers, to dread diseases as well as to useless accidents. Instead of floundering in their grief, some have chosen to get involved in church or parachurch work. Others have gotten involved in local crusades to promote research, or provide funds to build children's homes, or establish grants for medical students, or contribute large or small sums to needy home and foreign missions. Help your friend direct his grief toward a positive goal which can give him a new hope in life.

At some point in a person's experience with grief, he should rise above the lower moods that keep him imprisoned. Then he needs to lift up his voice, and sing praises, and pray to God.

Years ago there appeared on the obituary page of a southern newspaper this simple paid item. It said: "Billy, you know it was just a year ago today that you left us and the sunshine went out of our lives. But we turned on the headlights and are going on, and, Billy, we shall keep on doing the best we can until that glorious day when we'll see you again." It was signed simply, "Love, the Family." No names, just a simple public confession of faith. You can call it corny or naive if you like, but can you show me anything, anywhere, that is more positive and optimistic?

We must help our grieving friends do the same thing. When the lights go out in their lives, we must help them turn the headlights on and keep going. There are still people who need them. There is still work that needs to be done. There are still reasons to live. We must help our grieving friends discover these things and keep going. Jesus awakened the dead Lazarus and we must awaken the dead hopes of our grieving friends.

Few experiences in life offer greater opportunities to minister to your friends than those of grief. Follow the example of Jesus. Go to them, weep with them, bear witness to them of the hope that you have in Jesus Christ, and help them find a new reason for living. That's the way Jesus helped Mary and Martha.

EIGHT

Helping a Friend Cope with a Terminal Illness

I was attending a youth camp several years ago when I received word that a member of my congregation had just learned he had a terminal illness. Immediate surgery was recommended and the doctors were not sure that he would survive the operation. They didn't believe he would ever get out of the hospital. So he had a friend call and ask me to come to see him as soon as possible. When I arrived he said, "Paul, I've got to be sure about my relationship with God. I've got to be ready to die."

After we had discussed his personal relationship with Christ and he had found an inner peace about that, he then expressed deep regrets over his failure to set the right kind of example for his children. I suggested that I get his family together in their nearby motel room and that he walk over and tell them what he had just told me. He agreed and so I made the arrangements for everyone to be present. It was a moving experience as he told his wife and children of his deep love for them, his regrets about his past failures, and the peace he now had about his future.

It is always a traumatic experience for a person to learn that he has a terminal illness and should begin to prepare for his own death. Former Vice-President Hubert Humphrey said, "The worst and most shattering day of my life was the day I learned I had cancer."

And we never face a greater challenge than when we try to help a friend who knows that he is going to die. However, it is a part of friendship and discipleship for us to do all we can to help people cope with the prospects of their own death.

How can we do this?

The Five Emotional Stages of Dying

Dr. Elizabeth Kubler-Ross in her first book, *Questions and Answers on Death and Dying* (Macmillan), has helped us understand and minister to the terminally ill in a more effective way than ever before. She suggests that death is easy. It is accepting death that is hard.

I have known people who were absolutely terrorized by the fear of death. One lady who was dying of cancer said to me, "I am so afraid to go to sleep at night. I'm afraid that I will not awaken in the morning."

I know a man in his 70s who lives in constant fear of death. The first thing he does when he gets up in the morning is to read the obituary page of the newspaper and tell his wife how many 70-year-old men died the day before. He is so afraid of death that he doesn't enjoy life.

Dr. Kubler-Ross has taught us that there are five emotional stages through which a typical dying person passes. To minister effectively to people with terminal illnesses, we need to understand these different emotional stages. They are:

Shock and denial—the first reaction a person has to the news that he has a terminal illness is shock and denial. He simply cannot believe it and won't accept the diagnosis. This stage is characterized by the exclamation, "No, not me!" This is a normal reaction to almost any shocking situation. The patient often denies the diagnosis, pretending that he will get well and go back to a normal life. He may even go from doctor to doctor, trying to find one who will tell him that the first diagnosis was wrong.

Rage and anger—the second emotional stage that a dying person goes through is rage and anger. This means that the person can no longer deny his condition, so he feels a need to strike out in anger, frustration, fear, and disappointment at what is happening to him. This stage is characterized by such questions as, "Why me?" or "Why now?" or "Why not so-and-so? Wasn't I a good Christian?" In his frustration he may be nasty to everyone around him—his doctor, the nurses, and even God.

Bargaining—in this third stage the patient is certain that death cannot be avoided and so he seeks to negotiate with the doctors or with God for more time to live. This stage is characterized by the admission, "Yes, me, but . . ." The patient wants an extension of time to finish unfinished business. The Bible portrays King Hezekiah's going through this bargaining stage of death. The Lord told him to set his house in order because he was going to die. Hezekiah then turned his face to the wall and began to bargain with God in prayer. He reminded God of how he had walked before Him in truth and that he had done many right things. Then Hezekiah wept (2 Kings 20:1-6). He was bargaining with God for more time. In this instance bargaining paid off and God extended his life 15 more years. It is not unusual for any dying person to try to strike a similar bargain with God.

Depression—in this fourth stage the patient begins to mourn the fact that he must leave his family, his work, and his life on earth. This stage is characterized by the lament, "Oh me." Depression may be either active or silent. When it is active it is characterized by tears. When it is silent it is characterized by withdrawal. Jesus, who felt every emotion that we feel, may have gone through this emotional stage of dying when He prayed in the Garden of Gethsemane, just before Calvary (Luke 22:44).

Acceptance—this final emotional stage of dying comes when the patient accepts the fact that he is going to die and finds peace with himself, with others, and with God. The Bible is full of examples of people who faced their deaths with peace and acceptance. Simeon was an aged priest who lived in anticipation of seeing God's promised Messiah. God had told him that he would not die until he had seen the Saviour. When Mary and Joseph brought the Baby Jesus to the temple and placed Him in the arms of Simeon for dedication, according to the custom of the Jews, the old man said, "Lord, now lettest Thy servant depart in peace, according to Thy Word, for mine eyes have seen Thy salvation" (Luke 2:29-30).

The Apostle Paul was another man who was at peace with death. He wrote, "For I am now ready to be offered, and the time of my departure is at hand. I have fought a good fight, I have finished my course, I have kept the faith" (2 Tim. 4:6-7).

Naturally, not everyone goes through all five of these stages. Some people do not live long enough to move through all of them. Others refuse to accept the fact of their death. They keep denying death and either go from doctor to doctor or try every so-called "miraculous" cure they hear about in desperate attempts to survive. I have known of several people who went to their graves denying that anything serious was wrong with them. However, if given enough time and under normal circumstances, a terminally ill person will usually go through these five emotional stages before death.

Seven Needs of the Terminally Ill

Understanding what a dying person is going through can help you meet the basic needs of his remaining days. A dying person has at least seven needs:

1. Allow him to talk about his death. The first need a terminally ill patient has is for acceptance. He needs at least one person with whom he can maintain an emotionally honest relationship. He needs to have the freedom to share his feelings with someone, no matter how negative they may be. So be available and open to the patient. Don't be guilty of the conspiracy of silence by refusing to talk seriously about death. And don't try to avoid the subject. A dying person can and will talk about his death if you let him. You can say several things that will help him to open up, such as: "You must get depressed, discouraged, and angry at times. If you ever want to talk about it, I'll be ready." Or, you may ask, "How are you—honestly?" Or "Would you like to talk about it?"

When he is ready to talk about death, then listen to him. No answers are really necessary. He may be angry with everyone around him—including God. If so, don't feel that you must defend God. God can take care of Himself. If God laughs at the heathen who rage against Him (Ps. 2:1-4), He surely can handle a little honest anger and frustration from a dying person.

Remember that your friend is not angry at you but at the news—the fact. He is faced with a great loss and he is asking, "Why me? Why not someone else?" He is angry at what he can't do any longer. He is just venting his frustrations about pain, fears of dependency on drugs, or fears of a useless life ahead. He may be angry at the thought of not seeing his children grow up. Remember that such anger can be a blessing, a release. So stay with him. Be patient with him. He needs you. Allow your friend to talk about his death.

2. *Let your love trickle into him.* A second thing a terminally ill person needs is your expressions of love. During his illness he will experience great loneliness. Loneliness is not the absence of people, but the absence of meaningful relationships. Loneliness is the feeling that there is no one around who knows him or cares about him. While in the hospital, your friend may have many people around him, but may still feel very lonely. The patient must not feel deserted. He needs love and acceptance, not just television.

He will have an extra hard time facing death if he feels that his family and friends have given up on him. So reassure him of your love by visits, by words of appreciation, by notes, by flowers, and by gifts. Even when the patient cannot respond to you, keep ministering to him. You are a representative of Christ. If you simply listen to a dying person as he tells of a past fishing trip, which he enjoyed so much, or if you help feed him when he cannot feed himself, it is as if you are ministering to Christ Himself. Remember that Jesus said, "Inasmuch as ye have done it unto one of the least of these My brethren, ye have done it unto Me" (Matt. 25:40).

In her book *Scott Was Here* (Delacorte Press), Elaine Ipswitch tells of her 10-year-old son Scott, who was suddenly diagnosed as having Hodgkin's disease in advanced stages. The doctors gave Scott about two years to live. During that time Scott was in and out of the hospital many times for chemotherapy treatments. Scott started writing about his illness on his own. Then his English teacher suggested that he make up for missed schoolwork by writing about his hospital experiences. Doctors found out about his vivid reports and asked to use them in their orientation program for interns.

Weeks after his death, Scott's mother was going through his papers and found one headed, "How I Would Show Love." It said, "How I would show love is by being thoughtful and caring, helping in any way I could. Hugging and kissing would be a nice way too. Laughing and smiling when someone you love is happy, and being reassuring, and extra, extra kind when the one you love is sad. When you are very sick, it helps to have someone hold your hand, letting the glowing warmth of his love for you trickle into you."

So, tell your dying friend that you love him. And show it in every way possible. He needs to hear that his life has value and purpose and that he has fulfilled some need. You must not let him feel that if he died it would be as though he had never lived.

3. Help him hold on to hope. You need to help a terminally ill person hold on to hope. Tell him, "I'm not going to give up hope and don't you either. Keep praying. God does perform miracles. Tomorrow may be a better day."

This raises the question, "Should we tell a dying patient that he is fatally ill?" A Gallup survey revealed that 87% of the women and 92% of the men interviewed said they would want to know if they had a terminal illness. However, the poll revealed that some might change their minds if they were in fact seriously ill.

I personally believe that a terminally ill person has a right to know his condition. After all, it is his life. However, we need to be very careful about setting limits on how long he will live. Dr. David J. Peters, a 38-year-old dermatologist, was videotaped and interviewed just before he died of cancer. In his interview he said that doctors should not give patients "parking meter" predictions on how long they will live. He called time-setting a "parking meter prediction" because the physician says, "You've only got so much time on your parking meter," or "You've got six months to live." Dr. Peters advised against setting a time of death because the predictions of physicians are often inaccurate and self-defeating. He said, "I think you [doctors] make your patient become more discouraged. It can make him almost live out the prediction and then give up. And I think it is wrong. I think the easiest way to respond is to say, 'You are not a statistic. I don't know where you are. Some people are cured of this disease, so I don't know whether you've got 6 months or 60 years!' "

So, whatever you do, keep hope alive in the patient. Keep him looking toward the future.

4. *Help him have confidence in his doctor.* A dying person needs to be able to have complete faith and confidence in his personal physician and the hospital staff who cares for him. He needs to believe that everything possible is being done to meet his medical needs. It helps if he can understand what's happening, what the treatment is supposed to do, and how it will affect him.

Fear of the unknown is 10 times worse than fear of the known. So find out everything you can and keep him informed and confident. Doctors and nurses are often so busy that they neglect to tell the patient all he wants to know.

5. *Give him assurance about his family.* Another need that a dying person has is to be able to rest assured that those who depend on him will have their needs met after he is gone. This is particularly true regarding fathers and mothers of dependent children. I have

known several dying persons who were far more concerned about
the needs of their survivors than they were about their own deaths.

   6. *Help him know the Saviour.* Another need of a terminally ill
patient is to have a deep Christian faith. Like the friend I mentioned at the beginning of this chapter, the patient needs to be sure
about his own relationship with God and His Son. He needs to be
sure that he is ready to die. He needs to approach the grave with a
feeling of being at peace with himself, others, and God. He needs
to feel that he is not carrying regrets or unforgiven sins to the
grave. Many times a person needs to confess a heretofore hidden
sin. If a person so confesses to you, listen to him, and take his guilt
seriously. Assure him of your absolute intention to keep the
confession a secret. After the confession, assure him of your
forgiveness and that God's forgiveness is available also.
   The question sometimes arises, "Should I witness to a dying
person who is not a Christian?" You should. You would be remiss
in your duty if you didn't share God's great offer with him. A
person can be saved on his deathbed if he will turn to Christ. When
Jesus was crucified, two thieves were crucified with Him. They
were both terminal cases without hope. In those moments one
turned to Christ and the other turned away from Him. One was lost
in his dying hours; the other was saved in those last hours, so no
one should despair. There is hope for your friend until the end. So
you should share Christ with him and give him an opportunity to be
saved. Receiving Christ is more than a matter of life and death. It is
a matter of heaven and hell.
   You don't have to like death, but you don't have to be terrorized
by it either. Your friend will have greater peace and assurance in
the face of death if he knows Jesus Christ as Saviour.

   7. *Help him concentrate on living.* We need to help a terminally
ill person concentrate on living as long and productively as possible, not on dying. It takes such little time to die—just a small part
of one's life—a week, two weeks, a month—but the rest of time is
for living. So we need to help him make the most of the life that

remains and to live each day with greater intensity.

Orville E. Kelly, a 47-year-old newspaperman, was diagnosed as having cancer of the lymph glands for which there is no established cure. He was given the prognosis that he had from six months to three years to live. His first response was to give up in despair. He said, "To me, cancer meant death and death in a horrible, gruesome manner." He then went through all five of the emotional stages a person who has learned he is going to die goes through.

But one day a positive change occurred in his outlook. He decided to concentrate on living instead of on dying. He decided to live as long and as productively as possible. Help your friend do the same thing. Encourage him to consider each day as another day of life, a gift from God to be enjoyed as fully as possible. He will do better if he learns to live with his illness instead of considering himself dying from it. We are all dying in some manner.

Dying is never easy. And we must stand ready to help others through this difficult time. Do you remember the woman who anointed the feet of Jesus with expensive perfume, and how Jesus appreciated her concern for Him before He died? You can do a similar thing for your dying friend. And if you do, your care for the dying person will have the kind of meaning that hers did.

NINE

How to Explain Death to a Child

A few months ago I received a telephone call that a member of my congregation, a 41-year-old man, was at the point of death and that I was needed immediately. I was at the hospital within 15 minutes of the call, but I arrived too late. He was already dead. I offered what comfort and support I could to his wife and then returned to my study.

About 30 minutes later I received a phone call from a close friend of this family. He had been asked to tell the deceased's nine-year-old son of his father's death. He asked, "What do I say? How do I explain death to a child?"

About three years ago an elderly lady who lived with her son and his family died unexpectedly. Her son was out of the state on business at the time of her death, so her daughter-in-law called to ask me if I would visit with their eight-year-old son. He was quite close to his grandmother and he was disturbed by her death. His mother asked, "Will you come and explain death to my son?"

Have you ever had to do that? What would you say? How do you explain death to a little child? Explaining death to a child is one of the most difficult, yet important, tasks you will ever have to do, so you need to learn how best to do it.

Some General Recommendations

Nowhere is the conspiracy of silence more prevalent than in our dealings with children about death. Death education, even more than sex education, is something many parents don't impart to their children. As a result, death is seldom explained properly to children. This is because, I think, many parents want to spare their children the harsh reality of death.

But when the hour of death comes, parents are often so overwhelmed by grief over the loss of their spouse or their parents that children are left to fend for themselves emotionally. What a tragedy!

Death is a reality of life that must be faced sooner or later and needs to be explained properly to children. Here are some suggestions about how best to do that:

First, be understanding. A child's reactions to grief differs from yours. His experience is limited, and so he cannot fit together and understand everything that is happening. At such a time one of the greatest gifts you can give a child is an understanding heart. A child's feelings are worthy of respect.

A child's most common reactions to death are fear and curiosity. When someone close to him dies, he may be afraid and need reassurance. If one parent has died, he may fear that the other one will also die, and he will be left all alone. At such times what the child needs is to be held close and then you need to calmly talk with him, convincing him that no matter how he feels, everything is peaceful and undisturbed for the one who has died. And he needs the physical and emotional assurances that everything is going to be all right with him also.

He may be curious about what is happening and need explanations. Don't ignore the child at this time. Answer his questions as best you can. If he is curious about what takes place at the funeral home, he may need to go with you or another adult who can explain in a quiet matter-of-fact way what the funeral director has done. A child should be permitted to visit the funeral home and the cemetery if he wants to satisfy his mind about questions that are important to him—but not in the presence of hysterical adults, or not against his will.

Should a child attend a funeral? Certainly. It may be helpful to him, unless he is forced to go against his will, or unless there is apt to be some unexplainable behavior by some adults who attend. Joseph Palombo, administrative director of Chicago's Barr-Harris Center for the study of separation and loss during childhood, says that a child over three should attend funerals and burials and other religious ceremonies involving his dead parents. A child is an important part of a family and should be ready to take part in all significant family events. A funeral surely qualifies as significant. He should not feel excluded from any experience that is obviously affecting the rest of the family. However, he should not be forced to attend. The choice should be his.

There are real benefits for a child who attends a funeral. He can recognize more clearly that death has occurred. He can see that others are experiencing the loss too, and he may receive comfort, support, and expressions of love from relatives and friends who are not usually so demonstrative.

Second, be calm. How to tell a child about death is about as important as what you tell him. If you are composed, he will probably accept your explanation calmly. If you are hysterical, he will probably become hysterical and frightened.

When a frightened infant screams, we hold him close to us to give him physical reassurance. The same thing can be done emotionally and spiritually for an older child who feels that his world is falling apart. Some adult whom he trusts must be stable and calm as he talks with the child, convincing him that no matter how lonely and sad he feels now, everything will be OK later.

Third, be honest. Resist at all costs the temptation to invent stories to make death seem easier for him to accept and understand. Don't tell him such things as, "Your daddy has gone on a long trip and will not be coming back," or "Your mother has gone to sleep and will not wake up again." Explanations like this may create all kinds of fears and anxieties. The child may reasonably wonder, "Why isn't Dad coming back? He always did before." Or "Why did Dad leave without saying good-bye?" Or "If Mother leaves, maybe she won't come back either." Or "If I go to sleep, is it possible that I will never wake up?" Don't deceive a child in any way.

The single most important thing in explaining death to a child is to give him a simple, honest explanation of what has happened. You can say, "Your daddy died. He will not be with us anymore. That makes us sad because we loved him, and we will miss him. We don't know all the reasons why this happened, but we do believe he is with God now. And now that he is gone, we will take care of you."

You can tell the child with conviction that there is another life, where his father will go on living without pain or trouble. Even though we do not understand all about it, we rest secure in the belief that God knows, loves, and will take care of his father.

While honesty is important in dealing with a child, don't burden him with more than he asks. A child need not know all the facts; information should be geared to his level of understanding. The important thing is to be ready to give answers when questions arise. How much of an answer you should give is best determined by how much it takes to satisfy the child. At first you need not go into great detail. When the first answer no longer completely satisfies him, he will ask new questions.

When most parents first tell children the facts of life, they never give them a complete college outline of biology. They give truthful answers, but only enough to satisfy the child. You should do the same thing in death. But if you refuse to face reality with a child—to face the fact that the person has died, that he will be no more with you and the child, that you are sad about losing him—it sets the stage for mistrust and misunderstanding.

Fourth, don't blame God. A keeper of a cemetery was once asked, "What are the most common epitaphs found in a cemetery?" He replied, "The most common one is 'Rest in Peace' and

the second one most often used is 'Thy Will Be Done.' '' Isn't it
sad that we associate death with the will of God? We tend to blame
everything on Him. Untimely deaths are often caused by the
carelessness, sinfulness, and ignorance of other people. We
shouldn't lead a child to think that such tragedies are the will of
God. If we do, we may cause a child to hate God because he may
think God took his daddy away from him.

Some Special Considerations

Children react to death differently, depending on their ages and
their previous ideas about death. It will help if we understand
something about the way children of certain ages will probably
look on death.

Up to age three, a child experiences death only as a change in the
environment. He has not yet achieved his own identity and may see
the death of a parent as the loss of part of himself.

Children between the ages of four and six usually have many
spoken and unspoken questions about death. As they are curious
about the rest of their world, they are also curious about the death
of pets and people. To little children death is reversible. In their
play, the dead may immediately be able to eat and walk again. On
television they see people killed in one program and then alive in
another one later on. They do not see death as a final event.
Separation is still the most significant aspect of their concept of
death. When a parent dies, for instance, one of the child's first
thoughts is, *Who will take care of me now?*

A child this age may ask, "Will I die? Will you die? Why do
people die?" His reason for asking these first serious questions
about death, however, may just be the result of death's close-
ness—the loss of a loved one or a pet.

From about ages six onward, children gradually begin to understand that death is final and inevitable. Children this age have a
strong tendency to personify death. Death is a person in horrible
clothing or a skeleton who has come to take people away. These
children are most vulnerable to fears. They feel the loss intensely,
but they don't have the knowledge to cope with death realistically.

This is perhaps the most crucial age in trying to explain death to children.

Eight- to ten-year-olds usually don't like to talk about death. They divert themselves by keeping busy. They seem to handle death better at first, but they may be worse off later on. By this time they have developed sufficient mental powers and emotional security to acknowledge death as a biological fact which comes to everyone. At this point they are capable of expressing sorrow, a capacity which deepens through adolescence. Younger children are capable of only fleeting feelings of sadness; they are much more deeply affected by the reactions of others to a death than by their own internal grief.

Naturally some children may express concepts of death and experience emotions related to it that are beyond, or behind, the stages outlined for their age. These categories are helpful only as suggestions of typical intellectual and emotional stages of children.

Two important conclusions can be drawn from the preceding observations. First, children do think about death and are affected by it. Second, it is unfair to children to expect them to be mature beyond their years in relation to death.

Some Understandable Illustrations

It is important that we explain death to a child in a way that he can comprehend. One of the best ways to do this is to use the analogy of nature. Nature is a witness to the fact that all living things die, and that life comes out of death.

You might ask the child, "What happens to the trees in your yard when winter comes?"

He will probably reply, "The leaves turn brown and fall to the ground and the tree looks dead." Then you can point out that while the tree appears to be dead, there is still life down deep inside it, even though you cannot see it. It is just waiting for the gentle rains and the warm sun of springtime and then that life will burst forth from the trees in the form of new leaves and new limbs.

People are like trees in this way. Usually they live a long time.

Then something happens to their bodies and they die. It appears that all life is gone. Their bodies are then buried in the ground and we can't see them or touch them anymore. But just because they have disappeared doesn't mean they aren't alive or that they are gone forever. Though their bodies stop working, their spirits are still wonderfully and radiantly alive.

You can't see anybody's spirit or hear it or hold it or touch it, but you know it is there. The spirit is that part of us that makes us laugh, love, and believe in God. The spirit never dies.

We should tell children that as Christians, we believe God wants us to live with Him forever. He even sent His Son Jesus to earth to tell us so. Jesus died and rose from the dead and showed us that death is not the end of everything. Jesus also promised that He would prepare a beautiful place close to Him for the spirits of His people after their bodies die. This is an exciting promise! And one day, as trees that appear dead burst forth into new life, our dead bodies will come to new life again also. So even though you feel sad and lonely when someone you love dies, and you cry, remember that Jesus promised that all of His people are going to be near Him. And just as growth and new life come in the beauty of spring, so our loved ones will live again.

We need to explain that death is always the natural end of life. All nature, of course, is a witness to this truth. All living things die, but with us death probably is a long way off. We do not want to implant any fears of immediate death, either for the child or for us. The best explanation of why people die is age. By explaining death as the natural end of life, and old age as one cause, we can help a child understand God's role in death.

When an elderly person dies, it is easy to explain that the body is like a house that the spirit lives in which has worn out and the person cannot live in it anymore. At death the spirit leaves the body, just as we move out of a house when it is too old to live in any longer. Death is a wearing out of the body and a moving out of the spirit. This is a good biblical analogy (2 Cor. 5:1) and a child of nearly any age can understand it.

When the person who dies is younger, especially a parent, it is harder to explain—partly because there is no satisfying answer. The death of a young parent or playmate might well plunge the child into panic. Life suddenly becomes unpredictable; the ground is shattered under his feet.

As parents, we can always tell our child about heaven in pictures he can see in his mind. The descriptions the Bible gives are best. All the images of heaven that we find in the Bible point to our being with God, in His hands, totally secure and joyful and surrounded by His love. These are ideas we want our child to have when he thinks of God's gift of eternal life.

The traditional image of heaven, I feel, will help him understand that God's provision for us after death includes security and love. Just as we hope to lead our child to find that Jesus casts out fear in life, we also hope to help him learn that Jesus takes the fear out of death.

Remember that what you say and do has a marked effect on how the child thinks and feels. He must be able to cling to something strong and stable. He must have something truthful in which to believe. Then whether he is 3 or 13, he will develop the courage to accept this major change in his life.

Children accept death much more readily than you think. Their attention spans are shorter than those of adults. Soon after a loved one has died, they may be playing as though nothing had happened. Don't be surprised or disappointed at this. It is natural. Death is a part of life. Children can and do accept it amazingly well.

TEN

Making the Funeral Arrangements

When a person dies, the family's most immediate and demanding responsibility is planning the funeral service. Unless the deceased prearranged his service, or the family discussed and wrote down details, many decisions must be made in the space of a few short hours. Some of those decisions are: What funeral home will handle the arrangements? When and where will the service be held? Which minister will officiate? Who will serve as pallbearers? Which relatives and friends should be notified? When will the casket be selected? What information should be put in the news releases? Who will select the flowers for the casket?

If you have not been responsible for a funeral before, then you may not know where to begin. Two of the first people you should call are your minister and a funeral director he recommends. If you are living in a metropolitan area where there is an abundance of funeral directors, be sure you choose a reputable and well-established one.

A funeral director is trained to be aware of your needs and to do everything possible to help you through your distressing circumstances. He can make many helpful suggestions. Many of the details can be left to him. That is what he wants to do and you are wise to let him help in the ways that he has found by experience have proved helpful to others.

Your minister can also aid you. He understands grief and has worked with many other people with feelings like yours. He is available to help you with your difficult decisions and lend spiritual strength as well.

What Is a Funeral?

A funeral is a ritual of termination. It is a time to show honor and respect and to say good-bye for the last time. Since death is terminal, the rules of health demand that some disposition be made of the body. There are four ways this can be done.

The first and most common method is burial. A body may be buried below the ground in an individual grave, or above the ground in a mausoleum, or it may be buried at sea.

A second method of disposing of a body is cremation. This is more common in other areas of the world.

A third method, relatively new, is freezing. A few people are having this done, in the hope that in the future, scientists may find some way to bring their bodies back to life. While this is a fanciful idea, it is nonetheless an option.

A fourth method is to donate the body to science, and this is usually decided by the deceased before death because of the legal procedures involved.

Are Funerals Pagan?

In recent years the modern funeral has fallen under a lot of criticism. It has been called everything from "pagan" to "death-denying." I cannot agree with the current thinking that we should do away with funeral services. If we did, we would be doing away with something that gives those who remain a normal grief release. Though the intrinsic dignity of the individual remains the same, with or without a funeral service, one well-planned can enhance the perceptions of many who did not know the deceased too well.

In defense of funerals, people have always had traditions, customs, and rites for the important events of life, including marriage and death. If we didn't have funerals, we would invent new rituals to help us through the bereavement period.

Man is social by nature and needs support for the traumas of life. Man is unique among all of creation. He is the only creature of God that buries his dead. The earliest traces of man found by anthropologists indicate that while customs and rites vary from place to place and time to time, man has always had certain accepted funeral ceremonies. And the very act of burial is an evidence of human belief in immortality.

Though the Bible gives no prescribed rituals for burial, it is full of accounts of people weeping over their loved ones, buying tombs and burial plots, and being embalmed and placed in caskets. Joseph died and was embalmed. Moses died and God buried him in a mountain (Deut. 34:1-6). Biblical writers tell us of the deaths and burials of Joshua (Josh. 24:29-30), of Samson (Jud. 16:31), and of David (1 Kings 2:10). In the New Testament, we are told that the corpses of Jesus, Stephen, Dorcas, Lazarus, and others were cared for and prepared for burial.

The roots of many of our American funeral customs go back through Western civilization to early Christian and Jewish beliefs concerning the nature of God, man, and the hereafter. Those people who insist that all funerals are unchristian, pagan, and barbaric have a right to evaluate the services they have attended, but I do not feel that it is true of the services I have attended. God made man to be dignified and I believe his departure from this world should be dignified. A funeral service, the embalming and viewing of the body, and the sending of flowers is right and good.

It is Christian to respect a body. In this life a person is identified with his body so intimately that family and friends can scarcely dissociate the two. To honor someone's body is to honor the person. It is altogether fitting that we give proper respect to the corpse. After all, man's body is a supreme testimony to the creative genius of God. It was lovingly fashioned by God Himself as a suitable dwelling for His dearest creature.

Too, the Christian's body is the temple of the Holy Spirit and one day all those who have died will be resurrected from the dead.

Surely God cherishes the body, since He has provided His grace for this great miracle. If the body is precious to God, shouldn't it be to us also? I think it is altogether appropriate for Christians today to prepare a body for burial and accord it funeral honors.

What Are the Values of a Funeral?

A funeral is of course of value only to the people who are left behind. To them it has both therapeutic and theological values, or emotional and spiritual benefits. What are the values of a funeral service? What does a funeral service do? Why is it important?

For one thing a funeral helps us accept the reality of death. It reinforces the fact that death has actually taken place and that our loved one has gone beyond recall. Those who claim that modern funerals are a denial of death are mistaken. When a person is dead, there is no way to cover that fact up by the use of cosmetics and lighting. The person is gone and he cannot be recalled.

A funeral provides an opportunity for us to express love and respect, as well as grief, for our loved one. This is a necessary experience. A funeral provides an opportunity for us to say farewell to the body, with dignity and courage. The message, the ritual, and the gathering of friends are all aids in this.

Third, a funeral offers an opportunity for friends and relatives to gather to express love and sympathy and to act as a cushion or a support for those of us who are experiencing the pain of separation. We all need that. And we are grateful for it.

Fourth, a funeral is a public recognition of the value and worth of a person to the life of the community.

Finally, a funeral is an opportunity to bear witness to our faith. The burial itself is a testimony of our belief in immortality and the resurrection. But the entire service—the music, the message, and the way we conduct ourselves—can give a clear expression of our faith to the world.

Even the events leading up to the service can be of help to us. They can help awaken us to the total reality of death. The articles in the newspaper, the messages of sympathy, the gathering of friends and relatives, the moments spent quietly with the physical remains—all support the reality of our experience so that we can't run away and say, "It really isn't so."

The following are some answers to common questions about funerals:

Will I be able to control my emotions? You may wonder if you will be able to control your emotions at the funeral service. Don't worry. Everyone knows that you are full of sorrow and your friends will accept your feelings. If you pray and ask God to help you, you will be surprised at the control He will give you.

Should I allow my children to attend the funeral service? As a pastor I am often asked, "Should children go to a funeral service?" It seems to me that children also have to accept the fact that family members die. To try to hide this from them may create real problems later on. Children see make-believe death on television every day. So they may have problems recognizing what death really is. It is helpful for a child to attend the funeral and see, for example, his grandmother who has really died. If you try to hide the fact that grandmother has died, by telling the child that grandmother has gone on a long visit and you will see her soon, you are making death unreal.

Where should the service be held? The place where the service should be held depends on several things. It depends on the person's relationship with the church. If he has been a faithful, devout follower of Christ and active in the church, then the service probably should be held in the church. This would be more in keeping with the person's life and commitment. But one major drawback to having the service in the church is that it is often difficult for the family to return to the church for months without being reminded of the death of their loved one. I have known of a number of people who have had difficulty in getting back to church regularly because they kept seeing the body of their loved one in their minds when they came to worship.

Another factor in determining where the service will be held is the prominence of the person in the community. If he is extremely well known, the funeral home will probably not be large enough to accommodate the crowd. It may then be necessary to have the service at the church.

Is only a memorial service appropriate? One of the major objectives of a funeral service is to help relatives and loved ones accept the reality of death. When there is only a memorial service with no body present, there is no opportunity to look death in the face. In those instances when the body has been so mangled or burned or decomposed that the family is not able to view their loved one, the grief is much more difficult.

Just yesterday I buried a young man who drowned in a lake and his body was not recovered for 15 days. The body was so decomposed that the casket could not be opened. That kind of situation always makes it more difficult to accept the fact of death. Sometimes the question keeps returning to people's minds, ''Is that really my loved one buried in that grave?'' It is my conviction that the presence of the body helps to heal the hurt and further the acceptance of death.

How much should I spend on a funeral service? I have never felt it my responsibility to help a family make a financial decision on how much money they should spend on a funeral, any more than I would tell them how much they should spend on their daughter's wedding. It is wise for people to give some advanced thought to funeral arrangements and cost, but that is a personal decision.

The burial ought to be in keeping with the manner of life of the deceased. In making the selection of a service—the price of the casket and other arrangements—the family should be careful not to let guilt feelings cause them to spend more than they can afford. They should not jeopardize their lives later on by spending beyond their means.

Should I prearrange my own service? The prearranging of services is becoming more and more prevalent. People are making arrangements when they aren't under pressure and stress and can take a more logical view toward what they should buy and what they need.

What kind of music should I choose? Music is important in a funeral. It helps soothe the troubled spirits of people. It is much better to choose music for its Christian message than for sentimental reasons that may promote emotional excesses.

What if the body is donated to science? Some people have decided that all or parts of their bodies are to be donated to science at their death. In such cases legal forms must be filled out in advance and the hospital authorities notified immediately. The family will then want to arrange a memorial service within a few days.

What if the family has no money? In most states welfare pays a small amount of the funeral expenses of the indigent. But in most instances, the funeral home bears the cost. It is like any other business; they have to take the good with the bad, and they can't turn people down and feel morally right if the bereaved do not have the money to pay.

Should we have a service for a stillborn baby? Usually, when a baby is stillborn or dies within a few hours of birth, only a graveside service is conducted. It is not necessary to have a full-scale funeral. In such instances a brief message from God's Word and a prayer at the graveside with the family and a few close friends present is sufficient.

A Few Guidelines
A Christian funeral service is an important event. It should be brief, orderly, and dignified. It should include Scripture reading, prayer, appropriate music, and a message from God's Word.

Of course, a funeral service ought to contain, if possible, a good word about the deceased. But most of all the message should focus on God and the hope He offers us of the life beyond.

The funeral home or the bereaved can supply the minister with valuable information concerning the person's time and place of birth, family members, organizations he belonged to, and employment.

Your friends stand ready to help you in making your funeral arrangements. Don't hesitate to call on them. They will feel honored that you want their help.

ELEVEN

After the Funeral Is Over

After the funeral is over, the grieving family often faces their most difficult times. They have summoned all of their strength for meeting friends and family, making necessary decisions, and attending the public funeral. Then, within a few hours or a few days at the most, the relatives and friends go back to the normal routines of their lives.

Those who grieve are then left to return to their quiet duties. But their world is not the same. They have new problems to face and new ways of living to accept.

A few days before, they had many friends and relatives around them who were sincerely offering to help—but there was not much to do. Now there is so much to do and no one around. A new feeling of loneliness comes over them. The prophet Jeremiah gives a description of their feelings in the Book of Lamentations.

Lamentations is best characterized as a funeral dirge over the desolation of Jerusalem which was destroyed by the invading Babylonian army. Jeremiah, the prophet, had done his best to save her by his preaching. But she continued in her sin until the judgment of God fell on her. Now Jeremiah weeps and laments over her destruction.

In chapter 1, Jeremiah personifies the city of Jerusalem as a widow who is weeping and mourning over the loss of her husband. People are passing by, but they do not seem to care about her sorrow and loss. They are preoccupied with their own affairs and thus have no time for her heartache. In her despair and grief, she cries out to the indifferent masses, "Is it nothing to you, all ye that pass by?" (Lam. 1:12)

For months after the funeral, the grieving family may feel that no one cares about them because they see people coming and going, caught up in their own affairs. Sometimes they are even subconsciously resentful that others are so happy and they are so sad.

In these weeks and months after the funeral, bereaved ones really need us the most. Sympathy flows like a river immediately after death. But a month, two months, six months later, when loneliness and loss make their strongest impact, we, as their friends are needed more than ever. Usually by this time others have forgotten what the grief-stricken ones cannot forget. There is still much we can do to help our grieving friends.

Once Again, You Should Be There

Just being present is still important. You should stick by those friends who are grieving for many months. When death first strikes, the blow is so stunning that it results in shock. Through these days of initial grief and the funeral service, the family is often anesthetized, and only later does the awesome reality of what has happened slowly begin to dawn on them. During this later period of adjustment, they may need you more than ever. They long for a sense of acceptance, support, encouragement, and love. Nobody can live a full and meaningful life separate from other people. Grieving people need the strength, companionship, support, love, and encouragement that comes from others. To be isolated and alone in bereavement is one of the worst torments people can endure.

Every grief carries with it a distinctive loneliness. As their friend, you can never fully lift this sense of aloneness, but without such concern and interest loneliness is more difficult to bear. Support the family with your presence, your concern, your interest, and your devotion. Words may sometimes fail you, but a tangible act may express your supportive presence.

Bring them food in returnable dishes. This will make it necessary in days ahead for your friends to get out of the house in order to return the dishes, or it will require that you make a second visit to pick them up. You can drop by for a cup of coffee. You can invite them to join you for a snack, or to go with you on an interesting outing.

Late afternoons seem particularly difficult and so are evenings. Dinners in many families are remembered as times of sharing, and not merely as eating times. Specific invitations to dinner show that your offer is genuine. A ride to church or to a shopping center can be a healing act. Taking a child who has lost a parent to a ball game or fishing can show love; likewise cutting the lawn or shoveling snow for a widow can demonstrate your interest.

Be a Patient Listener

During these days we can also listen. A person in grief often wants and needs to talk about events in the past. We are inclined to avoid mentioning the person who has died, thinking that our comments will open wounds. So we usually talk about everything but the deceased. We turn the conversation to weather, sports, church, politics, etc. We seem to think that talk about the deceased will hurt the bereaved. Seldom is this true. It really hurts more if we act as though nothing has happened at all. Occasionally mentioning a conversation and a happy incident from the past can show that we too have loved and now miss the person who has died.

We should encourage a sufferer to express his inner feelings when he wants to do so. If we do not give our grieving friend an opportunity to express his emotions, he may withdraw, believing he has been rejected. Or he may push his feelings deep down inside himself, which may cause him emotional or physical damage later. We need to be willing to listen but not to judge. Feelings of all kinds may pour out—expressions of guilt, regret, hostility, fear, self-pity, depression, or rejection. This will be more therapeutic than we can imagine.

When a person has gone through a grief experience, his emotions are worn thin. It is then that he is more sensitive and thus more easily hurt than usual. So the time of grief can easily become a time of resentment. Other people can do things, or neglect to do things, that hurt the grieving person deeply. Let him talk out his bitterness and resentment. He may even tell himself, "I'll never forget that." You must help him forget. Help him realize that resentment is a heavy load to carry, and it doesn't do anybody any good. Talking may help release such pent-up emotions.

Offer Help in Finding New Interests

Sometime after the funeral, the sufferer must recreate new patterns for living that are not emotionally tied to the past. Though it will be done with reluctance, he must turn his eyes from the past to the future and seek new interests, new experiences, a new life.

As I am writing this, it is springtime, and I am sitting in a lakeside lodge looking out across a beautiful forest. Everywhere the trees are bursting forth with new leaves and new life. I have noticed that the buds of the trees are on the new wood. It is the young branches that produce the buds and the leaves. Trees keep their life by growing new life. In the same way a grieving person should learn to stay on the growing edge of life.

He should be encouraged to move out into activities as soon as he has the emotional energy to invest in them. These activities should not be distractions to keep him from facing grief; instead they come about as a result of having faced it.

C.S. Lewis wrote of "the laziness of grief." Grief does often immobilize, so we may need to help our friend begin again. Some people at this time seek employment. While volunteer activity may be available, a job where the sufferer feels a strong sense of responsibility to an employer may be more helpful. Meaningful and responsible work can be a sustainer of life. Enrolling in college courses can be a means of establishing a new, creative pattern for living.

Undergird your friend in his grief with the assurance that your friendship is durable and can withstand the strain, shock, and calamities which may pull against it. Help him know that you are not abandoning him, but rather you want to help him rebuild his life.

Serve as an Information Center

After the funeral is over there are many things your grieving friend will need to know. Usually legal matters need to be attended to. Since the average person gets lost in legal language and in small print, a lawyer may be needed to represent his interests. You might put him in touch with a good lawyer, if he wants you to do so.

Money is always a problem. Funds may be tied up temporarily. A banker may be needed to make suggestions that will help him arrange his financial matters wisely. That is the banker's business and he will be glad to give his services at such a time. Your distressed friend probably has a bank, but he may have no personal acquaintances among its officers. Your assistance in going with him or setting up an appointment may be appreciated.

Death often involves insurance. Most persons need insurance funds promptly in time of crisis. The insurance company's representative will help the family with the problems they face. It might help if you offer to make the initial contact for them.

Sometimes in settling an estate, real property is involved. Here the guidance of a trusted real estate person can be helpful in saving time, energy, and money.

Some people are uncertain about government services, considering them impersonal and tangled with red tape. This is far from the truth. The representatives most often do their work with a real desire to be helpful and understanding. They can help with matters having to do with insurance, taxes, and social security. If the person you are trying to help is a widow, she may not know any of these people or have the slightest idea of the help that is available. Your contact with them on her behalf may be needed.

It is wise, of course, for your friend to move slowly when making important decisions that cannot be reversed. Time gives perspective, and the passing of days makes it possible to see more clearly what is important and what is not. Many people have lived to regret decisions made hurriedly. So be present to help your grieving friend get the help he needs, but at the same time encourage him to move slowly in making irrevocable decisions.

Share Spiritual Prescriptions with Him

Finally, you can help the one who is grieving by passing on to him prescriptions that have helped you. You can share with him good books by people who have undergone suffering. There is comfort in knowing that others have traveled the same path before and somehow have found the clearing.

While you are recommending other books, do not forget *The Book*. The Bible contains the greatest prescriptions for life and for death. I just left the hospital where I visited with a lady whose husband is dying of cancer. He entered the hospital only four days after she returned home from major surgery. She said, "I was a bundle of nerves when I found out about his illness. I could not eat; I could not sleep; I just did not know what to do." She said her friends kept encouraging her to take tranquilizers, but she did not want to do that. Then she said, "I found my prescription in God's Word: 'Don't worry about anything; instead, pray about everything, tell God your needs and don't forget to thank Him for His answers' " (Phil. 4:6, LB). "That truth," she said, "saved my life."

This verse is a marvelous prescription for anxiety, worry, fear, and sorrow. These are all kindred emotions and the prescription works equally well on all of them. You need to pass prescriptions like this around to help others.

Look at the following prescription in detail. There are three parts to it:

1. Don't worry about anything. "Is that really possible?" Yes, it is. The answer to worry is faith. If we know about God's great power and love and believe that He can and will help us, it can save us from worry. Daily we should commit ourselves to Him. Then worry will gradually diminish. Faith and anxiety cannot grow together simultaneously in the same heart. One will overcome the other. If we strengthen our faith, we'll starve worry to death.

2. *Pray about everything.* Prayer is the greatest expression of faith there is. It is not only the way to salvation, but also the way of peace and hope. We can with confidence not only trust God for our salvation, but also with our daily care. We should share every need, every problem, every burden, every heartache with Him. He is interested in every need we have.

3. *Give thanks in all things.* Don't take daily blessings for granted. The more grateful we are, the more peace we will have. It is impossible for bitterness and resentment to thrive in a heart that is truly grateful to God. We may not be able to thank God "for" everything, but we can thank Him "in" everything. We can always be thankful that He is with us, and for what He is doing for us, even in the midst of the worst experiences in life.

I know from my own experiences that this prescription works. I am no stranger to depression, anxiety, and fear. I have walked in the valley of dark gloom myself. During a period of great emotional distress in my own life, I went to bed every night for several weeks practicing this prescription and I arose every morning, taking this great truth again by faith. The result was spiritual healing in my soul. This is God's timeless prescription for depression, anxiety, and worry. It will help your friend also. Pass it around generously and confidently.

So after the funeral is over, your grieving friend will need you more than ever before. Don't desert him. Keep going to him, caring for him, counseling with him, and having compassion on him.

TWELVE

Preparing for Your Own Death

After I had finished conducting the funeral service for a lady in her mid-70s, I stopped at the home to visit with her family. As we talked her husband said, "I never thought that anything like this would ever happen to us."

It's strange but many of us acknowledge that other people will one day die, but we live as though death does not exist for us or our immediate family. Our society constantly attempts to push the reality of death out of our minds. We do not want to hear about it; so we disguise it, run from it, or ignore it. Most of our life is lived in an attitude of pretense, when it comes to death.

Yet God in His Word continually reminds us of the brevity of earthly life and the certainty of death. The Lord told Hezekiah to set his house in order because he was going to die (2 Kings 20:1). Few people are given that kind of advanced notice concerning their own deaths.

Unexpected and untimely deaths remind us that we must be prepared for our own death at all times. Unless Christ returns to earth before we die, we must all deal with death—both the deaths of our loved ones and our own.

It is wise to plan ahead so that when your hour comes you'll be prepared. There are at least five ways to prepare for your own death.

Receive Christ as Your Saviour

The first preparation to make for your own death is spiritual preparation. You prepare for death spiritually by receiving Jesus as your Lord and Saviour. No person is ready to die until he trusts the One who lives forever.

There are at least five facts of life that you need to know in order to be ready for death:

1. God loves you and has a wonderful plan for your life. That plan involves your living in fellowship with Him and in obedience to Him. The One who made you loves you and knows what is best for you. If you will follow Him, He will give you both an abundant life now and eternal life when you die (John 10:10; 3:16).

2. You have sinned and are thus separated from God (Rom. 3:23). Sin is having a rebellious attitude toward God. This attitude leads to acts of disobedience. If you're not a Christian, you are like a light unplugged from its source of power. Sin has short-circuited you from God and there is no way for your life to be right until you are back in contact with Him.

3. You cannot get right with God by being good or by being religious (Titus 3:5). Once you discover that you are estranged from God, the natural inclination is to think that you can make things right by yourself. You may think that if you become well-behaved or religious, then everything will be OK. It won't! You are unable to save yourself spiritually. You need what only Jesus Christ can do for you (Rom. 5:6).

4. Christ is the one and only way to God (John 14:6; Acts 4:12). Buddha was a good man. Confucius was a great teacher. And Muhammad was a skilled leader. But Jesus is the one and only Saviour. He alone is the Son of God. He alone died for your sins.

He alone arose from the dead. If you have faith in Jesus, the Son of God, your sins are forgiven and your relationship with God is restored.

5. You must receive Jesus Christ by personal invitation (John 1:12; Rev. 3:20). The Apostle Paul says, "Whosoever [that includes you] shall call [that means pray] upon the name of the Lord [that means Christ] shall be saved [that's a promise from God] " (Rom. 10:13).

It is only if you are right with God and your sins have been forgiven that you are prepared for your own death. Right now you can experience that new, never-ending life if you will honestly and sincerely pray a prayer like this: "Father, I acknowledge the fact that I am a sinner. Forgive me of my sins. I turn from my sin today and I accept your Son Jesus Christ as my Lord and my Saviour, who paid for my sins. With Your help I will follow Him, serve Him, obey Him, and love Him all the rest of my life. Amen!"

The moment you pray that prayer honestly and sincerely, new life begins for you. It is a life that will extend throughout all eternity.

Be Adequately Insured

You should prepare for death financially by purchasing an adequate amount of insurance and updating it regularly. A few weeks ago I ministered to the family of a man who passed away in an automobile accident just 10 hours after his life insurance expired. His family was left not only to bear the emotional burden of his death, but also they had to bear the financial burden of his burial, plus ongoing expenses.

Insurance is intended to give you financial security for the unforeseen expenses and losses of life and death. The Apostle Paul told Timothy, "If any provide not for his own, and specially for those of his own house, he hath denied the faith, and is worse than an infidel" (1 Tim. 5:8). You have a responsibility to provide for your loved ones in your death as well as in your life. Insurance is one way to do that. You are not prepared for your own death until the loved ones you will leave behind are adequately cared for financially.

Draw Up a Will

You should prepare for your own death legally by having a will drawn up. Making a will is one of the most important steps in a person's life; yet only about one out of every five persons has a will.

A will is a legal document that states how our property is to be disposed of after our death. As adults, most of us spend about one-third of our daily lives working to make a living. We make money to take care of our needs, to buy things that we would like to have, and to accumulate a little money or property for the future. While we spend time and money during our lifetime to attain property, to use it, and to enjoy it, we should also give consideration to the time when our earthly lives will end. We should take time to decide what will happen to our possessions after we are no longer around to enjoy them.

Why is it better to have a will than to allow your property and other matters to be decided by the law of the state where you live?

First, a will allows you to dispose of your property—whether large or small in value, whether personal property or real estate— the way you *want* it done. If you do not make a will, your property will pass according to the laws of the state where you reside at the time of your death. Under rare conditions the results may be no different whether or not you have a will. But in most cases there will be a vast, unfavorable difference in the results if you do not have a will at the time of your death.

Second, having a will nearly always provides a saving of money in the form of taxes and other expenses. Both the federal and state governments have certain inheritance or state taxes which are to be paid at the time of a person's death. From the federal government's standpoint, a person with a valid will and a fairly large estate may be able to save a considerable amount of federal estate taxes.

Third, a will in many cases provides ways of cutting down or eliminating administrative expenses. After a person dies someone has to be appointed executor, or administrator, of the estate of the deceased person. Many states require a bond to be executed by the person qualifying as the administrator, or executor. And this bond must be guaranteed or secured by a bonding company. Naturally, bonding companies require a fee for this additional security. By having a will this bonding security can be waived.

Another advantage in having a will is that the decedent can provide in his will for the appointment of a person, or persons, or institutions he feels are best qualified to administer his estate. Furthermore, a will can also designate certain powers that the executor, administrator, guardian, or trustee might have which would help in settling the estate in an efficient and acceptable manner.

The will also allows you to appoint a guardian for minor children, in case you and your spouse die at the same time. Here again a guardian can be given certain powers to manage correctly the property left to minor heirs during the time they are under the age of 18.

Do not try to draw up your own will. A will is a technical and legal document. It takes a person familiar with the law to develop one properly. A person should no more be his own lawyer than he should be his own doctor. As someone has well said, "The man who does his own legal work has a fool for a client."

Finally, do God's will through your will. Your will provides an opportunity for total and continuing stewardship throughout your life and even afterward. A lawyer friend of mine told of a wealthy client who came to him to have a will drawn up. The man stipulated that the bulk of his estate should go to Christian causes and that only a small amount should be left to his two children. When the lawyer asked why he was leaving so little to his two children he replied, "I do not want to deny them the joy of making their own way in life. And I do not want to deny them the spiritual growth that comes from trusting God for their daily bread." Through his will he was both advancing the cause of Christ and trying to help his children. Had he not had a will, his wishes would not have been carried out.

Discuss Death with Your Family

You should prepare for your own death practically, by discussing death with your family and making plans ahead of time. Healthy families can and should talk about death and prepare for it in advance. As a pastor I suppose I am more conscious of the need for this than most people. My family and I have lived in a number of different cities over the past 25 years. The boyhood pastor I had before I went to college has retired, so I have no pastor of my own.

I do have a close relationship with several funeral directors. If I were to die suddenly, my wife would not have to make many of the difficult decisions: Where would I be buried? Who would preach the service? What funeral home would handle the arrangements? What music would be sung? Who would serve as pallbearers? I have already decided these things myself, so my family won't have to decide them at a time when they are least able to do so. I have taken time to write down my wishes in all of these areas, and have made sure several people know where this information is kept.

It is wise to make such plans yourself. You may even want to prearrange your whole funeral service with a local funeral home. What a relief it is to families who have had these decisions made in advance.

Make the Most of Today

No one is really prepared to die until he has first lived. So learn to make the most of every day that you have. Live every day to its fullest. You cannot control the length of your life, but you can have something to say about your life's width and depth.

Practice meeting God in prayer and meditation. And study His Word at the beginning of every day. Life is not all excitement and adventure. If you don't learn to find joy in the simple things of life, you are apt to miss it altogether. Life is not to be gulped; it is to be sipped. So take a deep breath, taste your food, talk with a little child, have a cup of coffee with a friend, sit by a warm fire, read a good book, take a walk through the woods, and enjoy a quiet meal with your family.

Do something for somebody else. Buy your wife a dozen roses.

Give someone a compliment. Call your parents. Write a note to a friend. Do a good deed. You'll get more from these things than you ever possibly give. No day is a perfect day unless you do something for another.

Live so that you will have no regrets. Years ago Ladybird Johnson wrote an article titled, "Life without the Presence" (*Time*, May 21, 1973). In the article she talked about her feelings and her life since President Johnson died:

> Invariably there are some regrets about vanished opportunities. There are so many things that I wish I had done, but I put my thoughts into two categories: The "aren't you glad thats" and the "if onlys." I try to keep the second column as short as possible. We should think about the second column ahead of time and savor things while we have them. To be close to death gives you a new awareness of the preciousness of life, and the extreme tenuousness of it. You must live life every day to the fullest as though you had a short supply—because you do. I said that glibly for years, but I did not know how intensely one should live.

It has been said, "Today is the first day of the rest of your life." That's true, so make the most of it! Then you'll be better prepared for death, whenever it comes. Death is as much a part of life as birth, and you should prepare for it just as carefully. If you aren't prepared to die, prepare today! Believe it or not, it makes living more enjoyable.

THIRTEEN

Questions and Answers about Death

None of us like to think or talk about death. Consequently, we have scores of questions that we are either afraid to ask or we do not know whom to ask. This chapter gives answers to some of the most-often-asked questions about death.

Can a Christian Commit Suicide?

Suicide is in many ways the most tragic form of death. It usually entails more shock and grief for those who are left behind than any other. And often the stigma of suicide rests heavily on those left behind. The practice of suicide is very old. Biblical writers mention six people who committed suicide (Jud. 16:29-30; 1 Sam. 31:4-5; 2 Sam. 17:23; 1 Kings 16:18; Matt. 27:5). Today suicide is increasing at a tremendous rate, especially among the young.

Can a Christian commit suicide and still hope to go to heaven? The answer is an emphatic yes. There is no doubt that suicide is a sin. It is a violation of both Law and grace. It is a violation of Law, for God has said, "Thou shalt not kill" (Ex. 20:13). The word rendered *kill* means "murder." This includes killing oneself as well as killing someone else. It is also a denial of grace. The first great statement of grace in the Bible was made by God concerning all creation and all life. God said, "Behold it was very good" (Gen. 1:31). Life is good because it is a gift from God. It is good and to be enjoyed. Suicide denies this by saying that life is not good.

But though suicide is a sin, it is not the unpardonable sin. There is only one sin in the Bible that is unpardonable (Matt. 12:31-32). It is not suicide.

Our salvation is not based on the way we die. It is determined by our relationship with Jesus Christ. If we are trusting in Christ as Saviour when we die, we are saved. If not, we are lost (John 3:16-18). The manner of our death does not enter into the picture.

It is my feeling that a person who commits suicide is temporarily insane. Since the instinct of self-preservation is usually man's strongest, to take one's life is an irrational deed. Such a person is to be pitied and not condemned. After all, we do not know how many valiant battles the person may have fought and won before he lost that one particular battle. Is it fair that all the good acts and impulses of such a person should be forgotten and blotted out by one final tragic act? Each one of us, probably, has a final breaking point. Life puts far more pressure on some of us than it does on others. Some people have more stamina than others. So our reaction to suicide should be one of love and pity, not condemnation.

Remember that our salvation depends on our relationship with Christ. He offers us eternal salvation. Not even suicide can change that.

What Happens to People between Death and the Resurrection?

Death is real. People die and their bodies are buried in the ground. That much we see. As Christians we believe that there will be a resurrection of the body at the end of time (John 11:24). The question then is, "What happens to us between death and the resurrection?" Luke speaks clearly concerning this matter. He tells us that at death our bodies return to dust and our spirits go to their eternal destiny (Luke 16:22-23). For Christians this means that our spirits live in God's presence (2 Cor. 5:8). Then, when Christ returns to the earth, our bodies will be resurrected and our spirits will be reunited to them.

Paul gives God's most complete statement on these future events (1 Thes. 4:13-18). Here is an outline of what will happen:

1. We die and are buried (4:13).
2. Our bodies decay and return to dust, but the spirits of Christians return to God (4:14a).
3. When Christ returns to the earth, the resurrection of our bodies will take place. Then our spirits and our bodies will be reunited (4:14b-16). We will have glorious resurrection bodies like Christ's throughout eternity (Phil. 3:20-21).
4. If we are alive when Christ returns, our bodies will be transformed without having to go through the death experience (1 Thes. 4:17; 1 Cor. 15:50-52).
5. We shall then "be together" and "be with Him" forever (1 Thes. 4:17).

Will We Know Each Other in Heaven?

Will we know each other in heaven? Most assuredly! The Apostle Paul said concerning heaven, "For now we see through a glass, darkly; but then face to face; now I know in part; but then shall I know even as also I am known" (1 Cor. 13:12). In heaven our knowledge will be vastly superior to our knowledge here on this earth. Surely we shall be wiser there than we are here. This means that we will know one another even better then.

When Jesus was with Peter, James, and John on the Mount of Transfiguration, Moses and Elijah appeared with them. These two men had long since been dead, so the disciples had never seen or known them (Matt. 17:1-6). However, without any introduction and without the benefits of photographs, they immediately recognized Moses and Elijah. This suggests that in heaven our knowledge will be so superior to earthly knowledge that introductions will not even be necessary. We will not only know our loved ones, but we will automatically know everyone else also.

The Apostle Paul also teaches that our resurrection bodies will be like the glorified body of our Lord Jesus (Phil. 3:20-21). Did the disciples know Jesus when He came out of the grave? Yes, except on those occasions when He purposely kept them from recognizing Him (see Luke 24:16, NIV). They knew who He was. They could touch the nailprints in His hands and the spear wound in His side. They knew He was the same Jesus. All of this together is over- whelming evidence that we shall recognize each other in the life to come.

Is Dying Painful?

Gregory Zilboorg tells us that the fear of death is present in our mental functioning at all times. Melanie Klein, a British psychol- ogist, adds that the fear of death is at the root of human anxiety.

Dr. Felix Marti-Íbañez says that the fear of death is rooted in three things: "First of all, fear of pain and the feeling of anguish that is implicit in dying. Second, the sadness of leaving our loved ones and all these things—work and joys that bind us to this world. Third, and perhaps more important—fear of the unknown" (*Reader's Digest*, March 1964).

Traditionally, we think of death as a hostile grim reaper, stalk- ing mankind with a scythe. Most of us tend to associate pain and suffering with death. We think of death as a dreadful experience. We often wonder, "Does it hurt to die?"

The best available evidence indicates that the actual act of dying is usually not difficult or painful. On the contrary, it is often peaceful and pleasant.

Listen to these testimonies:

In an article entitled, "How Does It Feel to Die?," written by nine competent physicians, Dr. William Osler said, "Most human beings not only die like heroes, but in my wide clinical experience, die really without pain or fear." All nine doctors agreed with this statement. Their concensus about death should give us a more positive feeling about death.

D.L. Moody was as mighty an evangelist in the last century as Billy Graham is today. In 1899, in the midst of a great revival in Kansas City, he became ill and returned to Massachusetts. A few days later he was dead. In his last moments he said to his son:

"This is no dream, Will. If this is death, it is inexpressibly sweet."

Robert Louis Stevenson, a great writer, said as he neared death, "If this is death, it is easy."

Eddie Rickenbacker was an authentic American hero. He first entered the national spotlight as a daredevil race driver. Then he became a legend as America's top flying ace and recipient of the Congressional Medal of Honor in World War I. Later he became a pioneer in the development and manufacture of automobiles and airplanes. He endured the most dramatic survival epic of World War II when his plane went down in the Pacific and he and six other men survived 24 days on a raft.

In his dramatic career he had many brushes with death. Seven times, he said, his toes were inside the Pearly Gates. Rickenbacker was a devout Christian. He was raised in a godly home. He said he had no fear of death because of his confidence that God had led him in life and had prepared a place for him in heaven.

On February 26, 1941, while flying to Atlanta, his plane crashed. For several hours he lay pinned by the wreckage in a cold rain. When he was taken to the hospital, he was more dead than alive. He held on for three days, encased in plaster from chin to toes. He said, "I began to die. I felt the presence of death, and I knew that I was going. You may have heard that dying is unpleasant, but don't you believe it. Dying is the sweetest, tenderest, most sensuous sensation I have ever experienced. Death comes disguised as a sympathetic friend. All was serene and calm. How wonderful it would be simply to float out of this world. It is easy to die. You have to fight to live" (*Rickenbacker: An Autobiography*, Prentice Hall).

What Happens to Babies after Death?

When a small child or infant is suddenly and tragically taken in death, natural questions arise. "What happens to an infant who dies? Is the child saved? Will the parents see the child in heaven?"

Though the Bible does not deal with the subject of eternal destiny of infants at length, it does give some comforting words. When a child dies before he reaches the age of accountability, he is safe. The death of Christ on the cross was an unlimited atonement for sin. It provided for the salvation of all people—for those not yet responsible for their sins as well as those who would become believers. So the young child who dies is with Jesus in heaven. And if the parents are Christians, one day they will be with the child and with the Lord.

David lost his infant son in death. When news of the child's death came, David said, "While the child was yet alive, I fasted and wept; for I said, 'Who can tell whether God will be gracious to me, that the child may live?' But now he is dead; wherefore should I fast? Can I bring him back again? I shall go to him, but he shall not return to me" (2 Sam. 12:22-23). Writers of the Old Testament teach that when God takes the parents home in death, they will be with their deceased children.

This teaching is also clearly expressed in the New Testament. Jesus said, "Suffer [allow] the little children to come unto Me, and forbid them not; for of such is the kingdom of God. . . . And He took them up in His arms, put His hands upon them, and blessed them" (Mark 10:14-16).

Bengel, a great theologian, wrote, "He had no children that He might adopt all children." The words of Jesus are meant to teach that we must have the characteristics of little children in order to enter the kingdom of God. But the emphasis is clear that little children are a part of God's kingdom. They have eternal life if they die before they reach the age of accountability.

We know that these children are safe because of the God we worship. He is a God of love, grace, and mercy. We know what happens to children who are taken before they have an opportunity to trust Christ as Saviour. They are in heaven with our dear Lord, and we who belong to Christ can anticipate being with them someday.

What Is Heaven Like?

I am often asked, "What is heaven like?" No words are adequate to describe it. The Apostle Paul once had an experience in which he was lifted into the third heaven. He was taken into the very presence of God. He said that this experience was so wonderful that he could not talk about it. Weak language could not bear the weight of what he had experienced.

While we can never fully explain what heaven is like, we still try. John, in the Book of Revelation, describes it as "a new heaven and a new earth" (Rev. 21:1). There are two words for *new* in the Bible. One means new in appearance. The other means new in kind. It is the latter word that John uses here. Heaven is not just this old earth renovated, patched up, and repainted. It is a new kind of heaven and earth.

There will be no obituaries or cemeteries on heaven's hillsides, for there will be no death there. There will be no broken hearts or sad good-byes in heaven, for there will be no sorrow or crying there. There will be no screaming sirens and no hospitals in heaven, for there will be no pain there. There will be no jails or locks in heaven, for all murderers and liars will be barred from it. Heaven will be a new kind of place.

Jesus also said that there will be "no more sea" (Rev. 21:1). The sea has always stood for mystery, turmoil, and separation. Before modern navigational equipment, men dared not sail far from the shore. They were afraid of what lay beyond the horizon. In fact, on the Rock of Gibraltar, someone carved the words, "No more beyond." It was believed that beyond the horizon was the end of the world. The sea was a place of great mystery and turmoil. People saw the waves dashing relentlessly against the coastline day after day, week after week, year after year. The sea was never calm, never at rest.

And finally, the sea represented separation. When John penned these words, he had been exiled on the Isle of Patmos for preaching the Gospel. It was the sea that separated him from the mainland and from the people whom he loved and with whom he had served for many years. When he thought of heaven, he thought of it as a place where there would be "no more sea." There would be no more barriers to separate him from his loved ones.

Then John saw heaven "as a bride adorned for her husband" (Rev. 21:2). A young lady is seldom more beautiful than on her wedding day. In all probability more preparation has gone into that appearance than any other appearance in her life. As the bride comes down the aisle to her groom, she is the personification of purity and beauty. Heaven is like that. It is the most beautiful place the mind of God can conceive and the hand of God can create.

And finally, heaven will be a place of meaningful service. Idleness is no divine ideal. The greatest hell on earth or anywhere would be to have everything to live with and nothing to live for. We shall not sit in idleness and boredom. The Apostle John suggests that we shall be engaged in creative, meaningful, joyous service for our Lord throughout all eternity (see Rev. 7:15-17).

So heaven is a place without sickness, death, and sorrow. It is a place of beauty, a place of reunion, and a place of meaningful, joyous service for our Lord throughout all eternity.

Victor Books for the Inner You

Do You Hear What You're Thinking?
by Jerry Schmidt
The Bible says that as a person "thinks within himself, so is he." Learn how to control the thoughts that control your actions.

Gaining Through Losing by Evelyn Christenson
This triumphant book shows how God can take the disappointments and tragedies in your life and turn them into unbelievable gains.

Healing for Damaged Emotions
by David Seamands
Satan uses many emotional problems to keep Christians from reaching spiritual maturity. Learn how to heal these problems with God's help.

Managing Your Emotions by Erwin Lutzer
You can achieve wholeness by learning to control your emotions —not letting them control you.

Overcoming Stress by Jan Markell & Jane Winn
Today's Christians are often exposed to greater stresses than non-Christians. Learn how to overcome stress before it overcomes you.

Putting Away Childish Things
by David Seamands
This sequel to *Healing for Damaged Emotions* shows how you can "put away childish things" and arrive at spiritual and emotional maturity.

Richer Relationships by Myron Rush
This book traces the deterioration of relationships, explains why they go sour, and shows how they can be restored at any point.

The Time of Your Life by Mark Porter
Jesus finished His earthly work without "scurry syndrome." His example and biblical principles provide time-management ideas that can help you accomplish more.